Successful Sales

Successful Sales

STEP-BY-STEP STRATEGIES TO GET RESULTS FAST

PAULINE ROWSON

JAICO PUBLISHING HOUSE

Ahmedabad Bangalore Bhopal Bhubaneswar Chennai
Delhi Hyderabad Kolkata Lucknow Mumbai

Published by Jaico Publishing House
A-2 Jash Chambers, 7-A Sir Phirozshah Mehta Road
Fort, Mumbai - 400 001
jaicopub@jaicobooks.com
www.jaicobooks.com

Original English language edition published by
Crimson Publishing
Mortlake Business Centre
20 Mortlake High Street, London SW14 8JN

SUCCESSFUL SALES
ISBN 978-81-8495-239-1

First Jaico Impression: 2011

Printed by
Repro India Limited
Plot No. 50/2, T.T.C. MIDC Industrial Area
Mahape, Navi Mumbai - 400 710

CONTENTS

PAULINE ROWSON

Pauline Rowson lives in the UK and has helped countless organisations to improve their sales and marketing skills. She is author of several marketing and self-help books and for many years ran her own successful marketing, PR and training company. She is a popular speaker at conferences and workshops and is also the author of the popular marine mystery series of crime and thriller novels.

INTRODUCTION

How can we succeed in business if we don't sell our services, our goods and ourselves? Simple answer, we can't. We are all in the business of selling whether we like it or not. Some people enjoy selling and find it stimulating, challenging and rewarding. Others loathe it. Many find it difficult to sell over the telephone and to cold-call, whilst others prefer this to face-to-face selling. Whatever your feelings about selling you are reading this book because you need to learn how to sell or you wish to improve your selling skills.

This book will provide you with a sales structure, tips and techniques which will help you to sharpen up your selling skills and boost your conversion rate. It examines how you can successfully sell both on the telephone and face-to-face. Part one introduces why people buy, how to plan for the sales call and the best way to get through to the 'decision maker'. Part two takes you step-by-step through the structure of a sales call, as well as the core skills of listening, handling objections and closing. Finally, part three provides extra resources such as a summary of the whole book, a question and answer guide to common problems, and sample structures of both a telephone and in person sales call.

This guide will show you:

- Some positive telephone techniques to help you get through to the decision maker.
- How to sell the benefits of your services/products to a prospective customer.
- How to plan and prepare for the sale.

- How to establish and build rapport with the prospective customer.
- How to use a sales structure that works.
- How to use the buying motivations to get people to buy.
- How to handle objections and close the sale.

Author's note: To avoid confusion and the cumbersome use of 'he' and 'she,' 'he' has been adopted used throughout this guide. No prejudice is intended.

PART 1

PLANNING FOR THE SALE

CHAPTER 1

Understanding selling

Unless someone sells something nothing happens – there is no business. Therefore it is your task to persuade or influence people to buy your company's products and services. You might persuade them to do this over the telephone or in a face-to-face situation. In this chapter we will examine the difference between marketing and selling, define the activity of selling, look at lead generation, and find out who and what makes a good sales person.

SELLING VERSUS MARKETING

Many people get confused between the terms marketing and selling. Often they think they mean the same but they don't.

Marketing is the management process of identifying, anticipating, and satisfying your customers' requirements, profitably. It involves putting customers at the centre of your business, understanding who they are and anticipating what they want, not just today or tomorrow, but next year, the year after, and so on. It involves constantly developing products and services to satisfy your customers' needs, and communicating the right message to your customers and prospective customers in the right manner at the right time.

In order for people to buy your products or services, they need to know about your organisation, which means you need to communicate with them in the most effective way possible. You can do this through a number of marketing tools. These include:

- Advertising
- Direct mail
- Press relations
- Exhibitions
- Seminars
- Your website
- Corporate hospitality events
- Email marketing such as email campaigns and e newsletters
- Viral marketing ie using social networking websites and other community based websites to build name awareness

You can also do it through **selling**, both on the telephone and face-to-face.

Defining selling

Selling, therefore, is one of the marketing tools available for you to communicate with your prospective customers. It is also a means of persuading or influencing your customers and prospective customers to purchase your company's services or products rather than someone else's.

THE TELEPHONE AS A SALES TOOL

Selling over the telephone has always been a popular method of informing and persuading prospective customers to buy from a company. The use of the telephone as a sales tool has many advantages, not least of which is cost saving. It is more cost effective to have a telephone sales force office-bound, rather than expensive sales representatives on the road knocking on company doors. A telephone sales operator can qualify leads before sending a sales representative out to a prospective customer to sell face-to-face.

However, not every business has the luxury of having telephone sales operators, and in many organisations the sales representative himself, or the business owner, is both the telephone sales person and the face-to-face sales person. He often needs to:

1. Follow up or generate leads.
2. Make appointments.
3. Sell face-to-face to the prospective customer.

TOP TIPS

The good sales person is constantly on the search for leads. And the good sales person consistently and methodically follows up on those leads.

Sales leads can come from a number of sources:

- Your company advertisements
- Your company mailshots
- Your website
- Your exhibition stand
- By visiting an exhibition

- By attending business functions: conferences, seminars, dinners, lunches
- Purchasing a mailing list
- Visiting industrial estates and business parks and collecting information on companies
- Recommendations from existing customers
- Referrals from other business contacts
- Through trade magazine and newspaper articles

ACTION POINT

List where your leads come from. Could you be generating more leads from other sources?

In order to convert leads into customers you will need to telephone them to either generate a sale over the telephone or to make an appointment for a sales visit. You might not be successful the first time calling. It could take you many calls over a period of time to get an appointment or to make a sale. It is important, therefore, that you track the progress of each lead and keep a record of when you called them, the result of the call, and that you log the date of your next call.

Make sure you have a system in place to follow up any leads, be persistent, patient and polite.

If you are cold-calling prospective customers by telephone, ie people who have had no dealings with your organisation in the past, and who have not made an enquiry, then you need to be aware that there are regulations in the UK on cold-calling.

Cold-calling individuals

The Telecommunications (Data Protection and Privacy) Regulations were introduced to protect individuals from unsolicited calls. Those who do not wish to receive unsolicited sales and marketing calls at home can register with the Telephone Preference Service (TPS).

The Data Protection Register enforces the regulations and has the power to fine companies who continue to make unwanted calls to those individuals who have registered with the scheme. If you are calling individuals in their own home, therefore, you would be advised to check out the regulations in more detail before doing so.

Cold-calling corporate leads

The Corporate Telephone Preference Service (CTPS) is the central opt-out register for corporate subscribers: 'A corporate subscriber includes corporate bodies such as a limited company in the UK, a limited liability partnership in England, Wales and Northern Ireland or any partnership in Scotland. It also includes schools, government departments and agencies, hospitals, PLCs and other public bodies.' (Telephone Preference Service).

These can register not to receive unsolicited sales and marketing telephone calls to either all their organisation's telephone numbers, or to certain numbers. It is a legal requirement that companies do not make such calls to numbers registered on the CTPS.

You can get further information on the website: www.tpsonline.org.uk/tps/.

If, however, you have bought a mailing list from a reputable list broker this will have been checked against the registers, and those not wishing to receive cold-calls removed from it.

WHO MAKES A GOOD SALES PERSON?

Before we look at who makes a good sales person try this simple questionnaire. Answer true or false against the following statements:

1. Good sales people are born with a natural ability to sell.
2. The gift of the gab is needed to get people to buy.
3. Shy people never succeed in selling.
4. Good sales people just have to explain what's on offer and people buy.

5. Good sales people can sell almost anything to anybody.

Now let's look at the answers:

1. Good sales people are born with a natural ability to sell.
   False: Whilst there are some personality types who find selling easier than others, selling is a skill which means, like any other skill, it can be learnt.
2. The gift of the gab is needed to get people to buy.
   False: The gift of the gab *might* persuade some people to buy some of the time, but if a person has been pressurised into buying something they do not want then it is highly unlikely they will buy from that organisation again. What's more they could tell others to avoid this sales person and this company and so spread a negative image for the company.
3. Shy people never succeed in selling.
   False: Sometimes shy people can be extremely good at selling because once they have learnt how to sell they often come across as being genuine and sincere.
4. Good sales people just have to explain what's on offer and people buy.
   False: It is not enough to tell someone what your company can offer and then expect them to buy. Customers need to be able to see the benefits of what is on offer and it is the sales person's job to demonstrate this.
5. Good sales people can sell almost anything to anybody.
   False: All right, so good sales people might be able to sell ice to the Eskimos, but if the customer has bought something he does not need or want, he will feel angry and exploited, and it is highly unlikely that he will buy from that company again.

So, what have we learnt from these questions and answers?

Anyone can succeed at selling no matter what their personality.

Selling is a skill; it can be learnt, practised and honed.

People need to see the benefits of what you are offering before they decide whether or not to make a purchase.

WHAT MAKES A GOOD SALES PERSON?

With the right training, and an awareness and understanding of others, most people can become good sales people. In order to be successful you will need:

- Professionalism
- An excellent knowledge of your products or services
- An awareness of your competitors and the market place
- An awareness of your customers' needs and wants
- Superb skills in managing communications, eg you will need to be a good listener and have the ability to ask the correct questions
- The ability to build rapport quickly and effectively
- Persistence

When selling face-to-face you will also need to project a confident image through your appearance and body language. In addition, you will need to know how to build rapport through your body language, and be able to read and interpret body language signals.

In respect of selling over the telephone you will need to project a confident image through your voice and be able to build rapport through the pace and pitch of your voice. There's more about these aspects in later chapters.

QUICK RECAP

- *Selling is a means of persuading or influencing your customers and prospective customers to purchase your company's services or products rather than someone else's.*
- *Marketing means identifying, anticipating, communicating and satisfying your customers' requirements profitably.*
- *Sales representatives and business owners often need to generate and qualify leads, cold-call to make sales appointments, and sell face-to-face to the prospective customer.*
- *Leads can come from a variety of sources.*
- *Selling is a skill; it can be learnt, practised and honed.*
- *People need to see the benefits of what you are offering before they decide whether or not to make a purchase.*
- *With the right training, and an awareness and understanding of others, most people can become good sales people.*
- *A good sales person needs:*
  - *Professionalism*
  - *An excellent knowledge of his products or services*
  - *An awareness of his competitors and the market place*
  - *An awareness of his customers' needs and wants*
  - *Superb skills in managing communications eg a good listener and having the ability to ask the correct questions*
  - *The ability to build rapport quickly and effectively*
  - *Persistence*
- *When selling face-to-face you will need to project a confident image through your appearance and body language.*
- *When selling over the telephone you will need to project a confident image through your voice.*

CHAPTER 2

Buyer behaviour and motivation

In order to be successful in selling you need an understanding of how buyers behave when making a choice to purchase and what motivates them to buy. This chapter examines buyer behaviour and the buying motivations. By understanding the thought processes that a prospective customer goes through before making a decision to buy, you will be better equipped to win the sale.

WHAT INFLUENCES SOMEONE TO BUY?

People generally buy for two reasons:
- Objective reasons
- Subjective reasons

In order to win the sale you will need to satisfy both of these. Individuals will buy some products or services to satisfy the basic **physiological needs,** ie to satisfy hunger and thirst, to be free from pain and injury, for security or safety reasons or because they have to comply with the law. These are the **objective reasons** why people buy.

But it is not always simply a question of needing or wanting a product or service to serve a specific purpose, or to satisfy that basic physiological need, that stimulates an individual to buy. The buyer will also be asking other questions about that product and service. They will buy for **subjective reasons**. These subjective reasons have a personal basis and are referred to as the **psychological reasons** involved in buying.

EXAMPLE

You are buying a car to get you from A to B, you may also need it to be a certain size because it has to carry a certain number of people. You have a budget and cannot afford a very expensive car. And you know that this car has to last you many years, as you can't afford to upgrade it that often. These are the **objective reasons** *for buying based on your requirements.*

Your decision to buy a particular model or make of car, or to buy from a particular garage, will be based on **subjective reasons.** *The subjective reasons could be:*
- *Will this car suit my lifestyle?*
- *Will it make me look good in the eyes of my peers or superiors?*
- *By buying this car what statement am I making and is that the right one for me?*

- *Does this car fit with my role as a director, father, mother, husband, wife etc?*
- *Do I trust the sales people in this car showroom?*
- *Do the sales people make me feel important and valued?*

Let me give you another example.

A brewery is selling a range of beers to landlords of public houses, clubs and restaurants. The landlords, stewards, and restaurant owners want good quality beer, at good discounts, in quantities they can store. They also want flexible and convenient delivery dates and times. These are the objective reasons for buying.

But the landlords, stewards and restaurant owners also want to stock a beer that is popular with their customers, which will bring in more custom, and make them look good in the eyes of the customers. They want to deal with sales representatives who are friendly and helpful. And they want to be made to feel valued and important. These are the subjective reasons for buying.

Whether it is a product or a service you are selling you need to understand why people buy – both the objective and subjective reasons.

Subjective reasons

The subjective reasons for buying a product or a service can be summed up as follows:

- To give pleasure.
- To give a sense of satisfaction.
- To nurture and raise self-esteem.
- To satisfy and feed an ego.
- To reinforce group identity, to give a sense of belonging.
- To satisfy the need for power.
- To satisfy the need for recognition.
- To satisfy the need for approval.
- To satisfy the need for respect.

ACTION POINT

Now examine the products or services you are selling. List the objective and subjective reasons why people would buy your products or services.

SELLING A SERVICE

The difference between selling a product and a service is that you can see a product, you can touch it, sometimes even taste it, but a service is intangible. It cannot be seen, touched or tasted.

The people who deliver a service therefore are a primary factor in the subjective reasons for buying. People buy people.

In order to sell a service you need to be both personally acceptable and have expertise. People are often buying 'a relationship'. Selling a service, and particularly a professional service, is highly personal.

EXAMPLE

When people buy an accountancy service they need an accountant to help them prepare and file their accounts or submit their tax return, which they need to do to comply with the law. That is the **objective reason.**

In deciding which accountant to use, however, they will choose one based on **subjective reasons**.

The subjective reasons for choosing a particular accountant will be based on the answers to the following questions running through the prospective client's mind:

- *Will he understand my situation?*
- *Will he have the technical expertise to deal with my accounts/situation?*
- *Will I be able to understand what he is telling me? Can I relate to him? Or will he make me feel uncomfortable by talking jargon?*
- *Will he and his firm be efficient?*
- *Will I be able to speak to him when I want to? Will he be accessible?*

In addition, the prospective client will also be buying:

- *The reputation of the accountancy firm.*
- *The image of the accountancy firm.*
- *The staff in the firm and the way the telephone is answered etc.*
- *The speed of service.*
- *Specialist knowledge.*
- *Cost.*
- *The personality of the advisers.*
- *The breadth of service available.*
- *Personal recommendation by peers.*

The accountancy firm, therefore, must make sure that it delivers all the above. If it fails to live up to the customer's expectation then the customer will be dissatisfied and will tell other people, thereby damaging future sales for the firm. So you can see that there are many individuals involved in selling the accountancy firm.

With a service you are buying all the people who work for that organisation, their attitude, their personality and their level of expertise.

ACTION POINT

If you are involved in selling a service examine the subjective reasons you wrote down earlier. Can you now add to this list? If you're not sure what exactly your customers are buying from you, simply ask them what made them choose and use your company. This will help you to understand what prospective customers are seeking from you.

UNDERSTANDING BUYING MOTIVATIONS

There are two sets of buying motivations that you need to understand before attempting to sell anything to anybody. These are the positive and negative buying motivations.

Most people you will be selling to will have the negative buying motivations foremost in their minds when you approach them, even if they have invited you into their offices or homes. In order to come away with the business your task is to switch them from the negative buying motivations to the positive buying motivations. I look at how to do this in later chapters when I examine the sales structure (see p.53). Firstly, I will explain how the buying motivations work so that you can see how they fit into the selling process later.

The negative buying motivations

These are:

I don't trust you

↓

I don't need you

↓

No, I don't think you can help me

↓

I'm in no hurry to buy – I'll think about it. I'll get back to you

↓

No, I don't think you can help me.

A prospective customer can run through all these negative buying motivations in his mind.

> **TOP TIPS**
>
> If you don't switch the prospective client from the negative to the positive buying motivations you will lose the sale.

Think of it this way: there is a knock on your front door. When you open it a stranger is standing on the doorstep with a holdall trying to sell something to you. You look at him. What is going through your mind? Is it something along the lines of, 'Who is this person? What do they want?' You're not sure about them. The negative buying motivations are very much uppermost in your mind.

Initially, when approached by a sales person, most people are looking for reasons not to buy rather than reasons to buy. Individuals are wary of being 'sold to,' often they are sceptical. If you don't gain their confidence at the beginning of the transaction then you never will.

So, let's look at the positive buying motivations to show how you can turn off the negative buying motivations in your prospective client's mind.

Positive buying motivations

These are:

I am important

↓

Consider my needs

↓

Will your ideas help me?

↓

What are the details?

↓

What are the problems?

↓

I approve

↓

You get the sale

There is also a final stage in the positive buying motivations you'd do well to remember and that is: **Remember I am still important.**

Having won the business you need to reassure the customer that he has made the right choice. If you fail to look after your customer after the sale then all that effort will have been wasted.

How to switch the prospective customer from the negative to positive buying motivations will be explained in the following chapters (p.53).

QUICK RECAP

- *Understanding how buyers behave will give you greater knowledge in the sales process and therefore make you better equipped to convert the sale.*
- *Individuals will buy products or services to satisfy the basic physiological needs, these are the objective reasons.*
- *Individuals will also be looking to satisfy the psychological needs. These are the subjective reasons.*
- *In order to sell a service you need to be both personally acceptable and have expertise.*
- *Selling a service and particularly a professional service is highly personal.*
- *There are two sets of buying motivations: Positive and Negative.*
- *In order to win business you will need to switch the prospective customer from the negative to the positive buying motivations.*

CHAPTER 3

Product and market knowledge

In order to be an effective sales person you need to have good product knowledge and an awareness of the market place in which you operate. This may sound rather obvious but I have come across many sales people who don't seem to know what it is they are meant to be selling, while others merely know the features but not the benefits. The prospective customer wants to know how your product or service will help him. It is the benefits he is buying. This chapter examines the features and benefits of what you are offering both at an organisational level and for your products and services, and what you should know about your market place.

FEATURES AND BENEFITS

Before we look at the features and benefits of a product or service we need to examine the features and benefits of an organisation. Why? Because it isn't just the benefits of your products and services that might tempt a prospective customer into buying from you, but, as we saw in the previous chapter, the customer might also need to be persuaded that your company is the best company to buy from.

You need to know, therefore, what makes your company better than or different to your competitors to be able to answer the question that your prospective customer might ask, 'Why should I buy from your company rather than ABC Limited down the road?'

ACTION POINT

Write down the reasons why you think prospective customers should buy from your organisation.

Quite often, in my experience, many directors answer this question by rattling off a hundred and one reasons why people should buy from their companies (usually these are all features) ending with a variation along the lines of, 'and we're really nice people!' Nice you may be, and, as I said earlier, people need to like you in order to buy from you, but *nice* isn't enough for someone to part with their hard-earned cash or their company's money. They need to be able to see the benefits.

The benefits that your organisation provides to its customers are its key selling points. It is what makes your company different from or better than the competition. This fundamental question needs to be addressed to ensure that your marketing is effective, and one that you and your sales force need to be fully aware of before even attempting to sell your products or services. The only way you can know what makes you different from or better than your competitors is to know what they are offering and where your organisation is positioned in relation to them. Let's examine this more closely by looking at an example.

EXAMPLE

A **feature** *of a company might be that it has easy access from the motorway, but what does this mean to the prospective customer? It means they will be able to reach the warehouse, factory, shop, office, easily and quickly, without the hassle of fighting through the traffic in the town. That is the* **benefit.**

In order to be a persuasive and more successful sales person, however, it is not enough to let the prospective customer deduce the benefit himself from your feature; you need to tell *him about the benefit.*

Before I show you how to do this let's just take another feature and benefit. The feature is that your company has car parking. The **benefit** *of that feature is simple for all to see, but you need to reinforce it to your prospective customer, by saying for example:* '**Which means** *you won't have to waste time driving around trying to find somewhere to park. What's more our parking is free so you won't have to pay, or hunt for change for the meter.'*

Here I have further strengthened the benefit by adding yet another benefit, ie free parking. And I can go on to summarise all the benefits to the prospective customer by saying: 'So to sum up you can reach us quickly and simply and hassle-free.'

Now let's put this all together.

Sales person: *'We're based just off the motorway, which means you can reach us easily and quickly, without the hassle of fighting through the traffic in the town. What's more we have our own customer car park, which means you don't have to waste time driving around trying to find somewhere to park, and it's free so no need to hunt for change for the meter. So to* *sum up, Mr Jones, you can reach us quickly and simply and hassle free.'*

Can you see how much stronger this is by stressing the benefits?

The two magic words which turn a feature into a benefit are **'which means'.** Unfortunately, too many people talk in the language of features. These alone do not sell.

ACTION POINT

Return to the list you compiled earlier on why a customer should buy from your company rather than a competitor. Make sure that for each feature you have the benefits of that feature listed beside it.

It is the benefits of what you are offering that persuade people to buy. Always remember the, 'Why should I?' question, as well as 'What's in it for me?'

Using features and benefits to sell

It is easy to slip into bad habits, the features and benefits become very familiar to you. You begin to take it for granted that everyone knows what you do. They don't.

TOP TIPS

Don't slip into the bad habit of talking in jargon. Jargon only antagonises people.

What you are selling can fall into one or more of the following categories:

- The solution to a problem they have
- Something that will fulfil a need in them or their company
- Something that will make them happier or feel good
- Something that will make their business more efficient, ie it will save them time and/or money, or make them more profitable, win them more business etc

In order for people to see that the 'something' you are selling will fulfil one or more of the items listed above, they need to be told what the benefits of buying that product or service will give them.

Here are some further examples of features and benefits:

Feature	Which means	Benefit
We have a wide product range	*Which means*	It provides you with one stop shopping to help save you time.
We have a large warehouse	*Which means*	We have the stock you require, therefore helping to save you time and hassle shopping around.
We have a fully computerised booking system	*Which means*	We are able to respond to your order/enquiry within x hours or immediately.
We have fully experienced staff	*Which means*	We can provide you with the right expert advice.

The customer wants to know what a given feature means for him and, by explaining the benefit, you will be identifying with the customer's needs more closely, talking his language and demonstrating that you understand his requirements.

ACTION POINT

Draw up two columns and in one list the features of your products/services and in the second the benefits of the products/services you are selling.

TOP TIPS

Know your features and benefits thoroughly before you go out to see a prospective customer or pick up the telephone to call them.

When selling on the telephone, or trying to get a sales appointment, keep your features and benefits exercise in front of you when you make your calls.

You may be asking 'why do I have to explain the benefits, surely the prospective customer isn't stupid?' Of course he isn't but there are two reasons why you should strengthen the features by explaining the benefits to the customer:

1. The prospective customer may not be able to make the leap between the feature and the benefit and by spelling it out you are helping them to do so.
2. If the prospective customer has made the leap between the feature and the benefit, then, by saying aloud what is going through his mind you are *strengthening* the selling point. This also helps you to build a buying signal.

BUYING SIGNALS

Buying signals show that the prospective customer is interested in what you are saying to the point that he is considering making a purchase.

A buying signal can come through at any time during the sales interview. Listening and/or watching for them, then capitalising on them can help you to close the sale and come away with the business.

Here are some buying signals from the prospective customer:

- He is nodding his head in agreement with what you are saying.
- He is sitting forward in his seat, listening to you.
- He is saying, 'really!' or 'I see.'
- He is asking you questions about your company, or its products or services.
- He is making an objection (more on this in chapter 11).

TOP TIPS

Buying signals show interest. You need to capitalise on buying signals by repeating and strengthening the selling point which has triggered this interest, and then add in another relevant benefit.

For example: 'Yes we do have ample parking, Mr Jones, and we're open until 6pm every day. Alternatively we can deliver to you. Which would be the more convenient?'

I'm now also closing the sale by asking the customer which method he would prefer. But I get ahead of myself. I will come back to this point and more on closing in chapter 12.

If you are not looking and listening you will miss these vital buying signals. Many people do.

Buying signals can come through at any time and should provide an opportunity for you to close the sale.

KNOW YOUR COMPETITORS

Effective selling means knowing who else is in your market and what they are selling. You will need to have some idea of the size of your market, of who is operating in it and what they are providing. In addition, you will need to have some idea of where your organisation is positioned in relation to them.

ACTION POINT

List five of your competitors in one of your main product or service areas. Make a note of the following:

1. What are their strengths?
2. What are their weaknesses?
3. Where are you positioned in relation to them?
4. What makes you better than or different from your competitors?

How did you get on? It is not always easy to answer these questions as the market place continually changes. New competitors will enter your market and your customers' requirements will change. You need to keep abreast of this and adapt your products/services, or the way they are delivered, to suit changing expectations. Continually research your market place and customer requirements.

QUICK RECAP

- *In order to be an effective sales person you need to have good product knowledge.*
- *You need to know the features of what you are offering and the benefits of those features.*
- *You need to examine this on two levels: firstly your organisational level and secondly at an individual product/service level.*
- *Prospective customers will want to know what makes your company different. Why should they buy from you?*
- *What you are selling is one or more of the following:*
  - *The solution to a problem*
  - *Something that will fulfil a need*
  - *Something that will make someone happier or feel good*
  - *Something that will make a business more efficient or life easier and more enjoyable.*
- *The two magic words which turn a feature into a benefit are '**which means**'.*
- *You must continually research and monitor your market place and your competitors.*

CHAPTER 4

Reaching the decision maker

When it comes to making a decision to buy something it is often not as straightforward as it seems because there can be several people involved in this process. For example, when deciding whether or not to buy a consumer product or service the decision can be influenced by a husband or wife, a partner, children, or even grandparents. In an organisation it can be influenced by many people from the telephonist to the managing director. Understanding who is involved in the decision making process and how to respond to them is an important aspect of selling. This chapter explores who is in the decision making unit and how to get through those called 'the Gatekeepers', whose job is often to keep you out.

SELLING TO THE RIGHT PERSON

Many people make the mistake of selling to the wrong person. They waste both time and energy, and in the process can also lose the sale. Why? Because what you say to one person will almost invariably get misinterpreted when it is passed on to another. So you need to check at the beginning of a sales interview that you are talking to the right person. Before I look at how you do this I need to examine what is called the 'Decision Making Unit' or 'DMU' as it is most commonly referred to.

The Decision Making Unit (DMU)

It is possible that you may have to go through several people in one company before reaching the decision maker. This is particularly so in the capital equipment market and if the product or service you are selling is an expensive one. But even if you are selling to the consumer, a husband and wife perhaps, there is still a decision making unit involved, as we will see.

THE GATEKEEPERS

Everyone knows the Gatekeepers! These are the people who think they are paid to keep you out, often the receptionist or secretary, or assistant or junior managers.

It never ceases to amaze me how some companies make it incredibly difficult for people to approach them. They treat everyone with suspicion and constantly moan about sales people little realising that their own organisation has sales people too, and is in the business of selling. Of course, we are all busy people, but by blocking all sales calls and refusing to see all sales people the organisation could be losing out on valuable services and products, and the chance to perhaps save money.

Gatekeepers, of course, have a valuable role to play within an organisation but they are not the decision makers, although they can influence the final decision as we will see. It is your job, therefore, to get past the Gatekeepers and reach the main decision maker.

You will more frequently come up against the Gatekeeper if you are cold-calling, either personally at a company's premises without an appointment, or on the telephone.

How to get past the Gatekeeper

Getting through the Gatekeeper to reach the decision maker on the telephone can be a bit like climbing Mount Everest blindfolded and just about as daunting for most of us. You might think it is nigh on impossible, especially in these days of call-screening, voicemail and answer machines. Admittedly these make it far more difficult to cold-call with the objective of securing an appointment but there are some things you can do to improve your chances.

First set your objective

What do you want to achieve from the call? Your first objective is to get through to the decision maker, but it is also advisable to be clear about your ultimate objective following this.

TOP TIPS

It is important to be clear about your objective because it will help you to project a more confident image. Knowing your objective will help you to sound in control and will help you to drive the call forward to a satisfactory conclusion.

So let's look more closely at some objectives for your call. This could be to get through to the decision maker with the aim of achieving any of the following:

- To secure an appointment to visit him.
- To obtain an order.
- To re-activate a dormant customer, and get them to renew their order with you.

- To mend a broken relationship, in effect to do a public relations job particularly if the customer has stopped using you because of a problem or poor service in the past.
- To cross sell another product or service.
- To up-sell, ie to sell a more expensive item or an extended warranty.
- To obtain information to update the database.
- To find out the name of the decision maker, and other relevant information.

Set your objective for the call and create the pattern of approach around it.

Make up your mind what you want from the call and stick to it.

Remember this is your call, you are in control.

Say this to yourself to evoke positive messages to the brain, which will in turn affect your body language and make you more confident.

Believe in what you are offering

If you have an excellent product or service, which I sincerely hope you have, then tell yourself this. You could really be helping the organisation or individual you are telephoning by offering them something that will truly benefit them. Be proud of your company and its products/services.

Don't hesitate

Remember, he who hesitates is lost! If, when you are calling, you hesitate or stumble over your words and sound indecisive, you will give the person you are calling the chance to cut you short. They will want to get you off the telephone as quickly as possible. They will not put you through to the decision maker.

TOP TIPS

The key to getting through to the decision maker is to keep your talking to a minimum.

You need to put pressure on the telephonist to put you through; it is their job to do so after all. The name of the person you wish to speak to and your name is all the information he requires. Don't respond to their questions, but ask questions yourself. Here is an example of how to do this.

EXAMPLE

You: 'Mr Brown please.'
Telephonist: 'Who's speaking?'
You: 'Harry Smith' (say this slightly louder).
Telephonist: 'Which company please?'
You: 'Is he in?' (firmly and politely)
Telephonist: 'Yes what's it concerning?'
You: 'Put me through please' (firmly and sounding important)

Alternatively you might come across this:
You: 'Mr Brown please.'
Telephonist: 'Who's speaking?'
You: 'Harry Smith' (say this slightly louder)
Telephonist: 'Which company please?'
You: 'Is he in?' (firmly and politely)
Telephonist: 'No, can I say who's calling?'
You: 'When will he be back?'
Telephonist: 'Not until tomorrow. Can I take a message/put you through to his assistant/voicemail?'
You: 'I'll call back tomorrow. Thank you.'

When speaking to the telephonist for the first time do not say why you are telephoning. Give your name and your company name, if you need to, but don't volunteer anything else. Why? Because every person you speak to away from the decision maker weakens the sale and will be misinterpreted. Take control of the call by asking questions yourself.

EXAMPLE

*Here's how **NOT** to do it:*

You:	*'Mr Brown please.'*
Telephonist:	*'Who's speaking?'*
You:	*'Harry Smith.'*
Telephonist:	*'Which company please?'*
You:	*'ABC Limited'*
Telephonist:	*'And what's the call regarding?'*
You:	*'We're a printing company and I want to know if he has any printing requirements. We offer a very cost effective, speedy service and can print brochures, labels, exhibition graphics, and stationery. '*
Telephonist:	*'He's not in at the moment. I'll tell him you called.'*

You've failed to achieve your objective. You haven't been put through to the decision maker. Worse still, this is what the telephonist is likely to relay to the decision maker ***if*** he bothers to tell him about your call:

Telephonist: 'I had this man on the phone today; he wanted to know if you wanted any stationery. You don't do you?'

Decision maker: 'No. If he calls again get rid of him.'

You have been completely misinterpreted and when you call again you will be fobbed off.

OTHER TECHNIQUES

It's all in the voice

Your voice is a very important aspect of establishing control and building rapport because on the telephone the vital visual element is missing. They can't see you and you can't see them. So use your voice to good effect. It has to convey an air of authority and confidence. Raise your voice slightly and sound crisp, efficient, and business like. Sound important. If the telephonist, or the person answering the telephone, doesn't know what the call is about how do they know you are trying to sell something? For all they know you could be the managing director of a multinational company about to place a mega order, or a very important customer!

ACTION POINT

Think of yourself as the managing director of a large organisation, responsible for many staff and making important decisions. Now think about how you would sound and what your body language would be like. Try imagining yourself in this role. Test it out by pretending to make a few dummy calls with no one on the other end of the line and record your voice.

Alternatively, imagine you are an aggressive customer. How does your voice sound then? Curt, abrupt, determined, important? Try experimenting with your voice to get the command in it you require.

TOP TIPS

Remember the person on the other end of the telephone can't see you. All they have to judge you on is your voice – so use it.

Use your position

If you are a managing director, head teacher, chief executive or someone who holds a senior position in an organisation (even if it is a very small organisation) then use your position to get through the Gatekeeper. Give your name, position and company name and no more.

What's in a name?

Quite a lot actually. Let's just examine how you use your name. If you say, 'Hi, I'm Mandy from ABC Limited' in a little girl singsong voice, or 'Hi, I'm Matt from ABC Limited,' in a sales voice, the automatic reaction of the person who has answered the telephone is 'what are you selling?' The blocks will immediately go up.

If you are a married woman then try using your title and your surname, for example I would say Mrs Rowson. This automatically carries more authority and could imply that you are a customer.

EXAMPLE

A company offering storage facilities to organisations embarked on a telephone sales campaign, calling businesses. When the telephone sales staff changed their technique from just giving their first names and the company name to announcing themselves more formally either as Miss, Ms or Mrs or Mr, their success rate in getting through to the decision maker rose considerably.

A man can use his salutation and his surname or simply his surname; 'Smith,' said curtly often gets them put through. If you don't want to use the salutation then simply giving your full name, both first name and surname can work. And if you are known by the shortened version of your name then try using the full version, for example: Matthew instead of Matt, James instead of Jim, Victoria rather than Vicky, Amanda rather than Mandy.

ACTION POINT

Try the different approaches mentioned above and monitor the results. See what works best for you and for the types of customers/organisations you are calling.

Try calling at different times

If you have difficulty getting past a particular telephonist then try calling at a different time of the day, for example the lunch period when the relief receptionist might be on duty and might not be so efficient or thorough as the full time one.

Try calling later in the day, after hours for example, when the system is switched over to night service. You may find yourself sailing through, or even talking directly to the person you require. This is obviously dependent on knowing the working patterns of the industry you are calling.

Use powerful words

'I really do ***need*** to speak to him'. **Need** is the key word here, it implies urgency and people often respond positively to it.

Put pressure on the telephonist

Another last ditch technique, if you are really being blocked, but one that works, is to ask for the receptionist/telephonist's name and so put the pressure on him. When he asks why you need this information, tell him that when Mr Brown contacts your organisation in the future, you will say that the decision not to buy was made by the telephonist. You will soon be put through if they think they are taking responsibility.

EXAMPLE

Emma was calling the managing director of a company to offer him free training places on a course run by a government organisation. She also wanted to tell the managing director that free business advice was also available. She had tried several times to speak to the managing director but was blocked on every opportunity. Exasperated at not being given the chance to tell the managing director what was on offer she asked for the telephonist's name and told her that she would inform the managing director by other means that he had lost his chance of free training and free business advice. She was then swiftly and grudgingly put through. The managing director was delighted with the offer and took up both the free training and the free business advice.

Getting past a second Gatekeeper

So, having got through the telephonist, what happens if you then get put through to the secretary or assistant, who is also a Gatekeeper?

Again the golden rule is to keep your talking to a minimum. By the nature of the situation he is asking you the questions so again try to reverse this by asking questions yourself. Take a slightly more gentle approach, because you might also need this person as an ally in the decision making process.

EXAMPLE

You:	*'May I speak to Mr Brown please?'*
Secretary:	*'What's it concerning?'*
You:	*'Is he in?'*
Secretary:	*'No. He's out on business at the moment. What's it about?'*
You:	*'Can you tell me when he will be back?'*
Secretary:	*'About 3pm. What's it concerning?'*
You:	*'Thanks for your help. I'll ring him back at three.'*

Put pressure on the secretary or assistant, control the conversation, but be polite. You need to very quickly judge how much information you can give to this person. And while you should not say too much you might judge that this person really is the power behind the throne, so you might need to tell him more. Only you will be able to decide this.

Perhaps on the first time of speaking to him keep your information to a minimum, but if you continually have difficulty in getting past this person to reach the ultimate decision maker, you might need to give him more information. In this case try and use this person as an ally in helping you to speak to the decision maker. Take time to be friendly and professional, tell him why you need to speak to the decision maker, ie you believe you have something that can help the company save time or money etc but don't go into reams of detail. Don't be too pushy, treat them with respect and see if you can get them to suggest when might be the best time to call back.

If the decision maker is on the other line, hold on or call back later. Retain the initiative. Don't get into the situation where they ask you to send a brochure and telephone later. This is the fob off. And don't leave messages on voicemail or answer machines, they won't be returned.

OTHERS IN THE DECISION MAKING UNIT (DMU)

The other people who are a part of the DMU are:

Users

These are people who may use the piece of machinery, the computer software, or the equipment or systems you are selling. They could therefore influence the purchasing decision by telling the main decision maker what they like and don't like about a product or a service, and what they like and dislike about you!

Those authorising the purchase may ask the Users for their opinion. Users could also have an affect on future sales and whether the goods or services purchased were actually value for money and worked satisfactorily.

Influencers

These are sometimes more difficult to spot. They may not obviously be involved in the buying process but they may influence it. They could even be outsiders who have heard of your company and its reputation and either endorse it or slate it to the decision maker.

You might also find that your Gatekeeper is in fact also an Influencer, for example the person on the security gate is the managing director's father, and the receptionist is the managing director's partner. If they didn't like you then you could find yourself without a sale.

In a transaction of consumer goods one partner may be buying a piece of equipment but the other partner may well have considerable influence on the decision to buy. For example, how many car sales people have got it wrong by selling only to the man in a transaction and ignoring the woman? They have underestimated the influence of the woman in the decision making unit.

EXAMPLE

I was involved in training some sales people who worked at the luxury end of the motorboat market. These boats retailed for £250,000 upwards. Many of the buyers were men who were quite often accompanied by a female partner and sometimes by children. Whilst it is always wrong to make assumptions I will nevertheless make one here and say that our man was looking for speed and performance from the motorboat whilst the woman was looking for comfort, spaciousness and interior design. The sales people would be quite wrong to ignore the concerns and views of the woman and the children in this situation who can strongly influence the decision to buy this type or make of boat. If they did they could risk losing a sale.

Buyers

These are professional people within the organisation, a purchasing manager or buyer, whose job it is to source and buy on behalf of the business. They are paid to get the best deal. Generally speaking, they will be tough and thorough negotiators. They can often be the most difficult people to sell to because of this.

Deciders

Who decides on whether or not to buy can depend on the value of the transaction. Decisions to purchase may be taken lower down the line for low cost or routine purchases, for example a secretary, assistant, store person or manager. But they are usually taken at a higher level where big money is involved, for example at director level.

Specifiers

These are people such as architects or engineers. People who will specify materials or components needed to meet the requirements for a specific project. Specifiers may have to be convinced at an early stage that a specification embracing your product will satisfy their needs.

> Finding the right person to sell to, or going through the various people in the DMU, requires a methodical and persistent approach.

So how do you know if the person you are seeing face-to-face is the decision maker? Simple; ask them, and ask them right at the beginning of the meeting. For example ask 'Would anyone else be involved in the decision to buy?' or 'Who else needs to be involved if you decide to go ahead?' This will help you to establish if you need to involve anyone else in the sales presentation, or if you need to return to make another sales presentation.

If the person you are seeing reveals that he is not the final decision maker, ask if the decision maker is available to join the meeting. If they are not available then continue with the sales interview. It would be impolite to terminate it so abruptly and you do not know how much influence the person you are seeing has with the decision maker. Try and determine this and adjust your sales pitch accordingly. Ensure that before you leave you make another appointment to return when you can see both the decision maker and anyone else involved in the buying decision.

If you don't know who the decision maker is when making a telephone sales call, or you are uncertain who would be the best person to speak to, then make two calls: the first to get information and establish the correct person to contact, and the second call to ask for him or her by name. That way you stand a much better chance of being put through, particularly if you use some of the techniques previously described to help you.

QUICK RECAP

- *You may have to go through several people in one company before reaching the decision maker, this is called the Decision Making Unit (DMU).*
- *The Gatekeepers are the people who think they are paid to keep you out.*
- *Your first objective is to get through to the decision maker; be clear about this from the start as it will show through in your voice.*
- *Every person you speak to away from the decision maker weakens the sale and what you have said will be misinterpreted.*
- *Finding the right person to sell to, or going through the various people in the DMU, requires a methodical and persistent approach.*
- *Ask if the person you are seeing is the decision maker. This will help you to establish if you need to involve anyone else in the sales presentation, or if you need to return to make another sales presentation.*

CHAPTER 5

Preparing for the sales call and visit

There is an old saying, 'If you fail to prepare then you prepare to fail.' Understanding what motivates your customers to buy, knowing your products and your market place, is all part of the pre-sales research but there is more you need to do before you lift the telephone to make that call or visit your prospective customer. This chapter examines how to prepare for the sales call and visit. It includes planning your calls and visits, setting targets and objectives, and conducting other pre-sales research.

PLAN WHEN TO MAKE YOUR SALES CALLS

Firstly, you will need to look at *who* you are targeting and then plan *when* will be the most appropriate time to telephone or visit them. You need to know this because different groups of customers will be available at varying times throughout the day.

EXAMPLE

A sales person needed to telephone restaurants to get appointments. When he called between 12 noon and 2.30pm he failed to speak to the decision maker, who was the restaurant manager. However, when he called mid-morning and mid-afternoon he was far more successful. This was because the restaurants were too busy to take his telephone call during the lunch period.

If you are calling a medical practice to speak to the practice manager or a GP then it is pointless calling them between 9am and 11am and between 4.30pm and 7pm, because they will be very busy taking calls and seeing patients.

The same applies for the sales visit. You are hardly likely to get the best results if you visit the prospective customer at the busiest time of the day for him. Rather obvious you might think but it happens.

TOP TIPS

The more you know about the industries you are targeting and their practices the more informed you will be about the best times to call them.

GROUP YOUR PROSPECTIVE CUSTOMERS

This is more critical for the telephone sales calls than the sales visits, though it makes sense to conduct your sales visits by geographical area and therefore save time and petrol expenses.

Putting your prospective customers into easily identifiable groups will help you plan your telephone sales calls and measure and analyse the results. You will be able to see which calls are the most successful, and which groups give you the best results. You can group your prospective customers in a number of ways, either by:

- Industry type
- Geographical area
- Existing customers
- Dormant customers

For example, you might decide to target a geographical area for one week with the aim of securing some appointments in that one area for the following week, thereby maximising your time and minimising travel costs. Or you could target a particular industry sector one week and another the following week and then measure and compare results. From this you might be able to decide which sector is more worthwhile targeting.

Alternatively, you might decide to target existing customers one day with the aim of cross selling or up-selling to them and then call prospective customers the next day with the aim of getting an order or generating a sales visit. Or you could spend a week or a day calling dormant customers with the purpose of reactivating the accounts.

ACTION POINT

Examine the organisations you need to telephone. Try and group them into easily identifiable sectors by industry type, area or customer/past customer. Decide when will be the most productive time to call them. Draw up a timetable for calling them, specifying the group you are going to target and which days and/or weeks you are going to telephone them.

SETTING CALL TARGETS

Be realistic about how many telephone sales calls or sales visits you can make in one day. If you are arranging sales visits then allow time for traffic and travel disruption. Can you make some telephone calls in between visits when there is a bigger time gap?

When setting targets be careful not to put too much emphasis on the number of sales appointments to be made. This can lead to you being so concerned with securing the appointment that you put unnecessary pressure on the prospective customer. In this event you could find yourself going out on a false errand if the lead has not been properly qualified, thereby wasting time and money. It can also alienate the prospective customer from having further dealings with your company because no one likes being bullied and pressured into agreeing to a sales visit.

TOP TIPS

If you are making sales appointments it is better to make good, qualified appointments rather than making those just to get the numbers to reach targets.

ACTION POINT

Draw up a schedule of how many calls to make a day or a week. Set yourself targets for the number of calls to be made but make sure this is a realistic target.

SETTING OBJECTIVES

It is important that you are clear about your objectives for the telephone sales call and the sales visit from the outset. This helps to focus your mind and enables you to drive your sales structure to the desired close.

Before telephoning or visiting the prospective customer be clear about your objective.

We've already examined objective setting for the telephone sales call in chapter 4, but to recap this can be:

- To get through to the decision maker with the aim of securing an appointment to visit him or obtaining an order.
- To re-activate a dormant customer, and get them to renew their order with you.
- To do a public relations job, particularly if the customer has stopped using you because of a problem or bad service in the past.
- To cross sell another product or service.
- To up-sell, ie to sell a more expensive item or an extended warranty.
- To obtain information to update the database.
- To find the name of the decision maker, and other relevant information.

Objectives for the sales visit

Be clear what you want to achieve from the sales visit. Is it to come away with the business or the order? Is this achievable for your type of product or service? The higher the value of the purchase the longer it will take to get the sale. So, although you might like to get an order on that first visit, it might not be a totally realistic objective. In this case, you need to ensure that you are able to return. This could be after the prospective customer has consulted others in his company, checked his budget, undertaken a trial, or gained further testimonials from your existing customers, or all of these.

In addition, the prospective customer might be locked into a contract with his existing suppliers, which cannot be terminated for some time. In this situation you need to ensure that you maintain contact with the prospective customer and continue to build a good relationship with him.

You might also discover on that first sales visit that there are others involved in the Decision Making Unit (DMU). You may need to return to the company to demonstrate equipment or to give a presentation.

I look at objection handling in chapter 11, but if the customer does not wish to buy from you, always try to leave the door open to go back in later. You never know when things might change.

Write down the objectives for your telephone sales calls or sales visits. If you are targeting different groups of customers, write the objective for each group beside them.

PRE-SALES RESEARCH

Before visiting (and even telephoning) the prospective customer, try to gain as much information about them as possible. You can do this by:

- Talking to your colleagues
- Talking to your suppliers and contacts
- Reviewing any press items about them in the newspapers or trade journals
- Conducting a search on the internet
- Viewing the prospective customer's website
- Conducting a company search and undertaking a credit rating

TOP TIPS

By using this background information when speaking to the prospective customer you will show interest in that customer, knowledge of his sector and needs, and you will also help to satisfy two of those positive buying motivations: 'I am important' and 'Consider my needs'.

Before visiting the prospective customer make sure you have all the relevant literature to hand. This can include:

- Leaflets, price lists and brochures
- Customer testimonials
- Samples
- Business cards or your contact details
- A list of features and benefits ready to refresh yourself before calling or visiting the prospective customer

Prepare as well as you can before any sales interview. The more you know about your prospective customers and their needs the more successful you will be.

QUICK RECAP

- *Plan who you are targeting.*
- *Putting your target audience into easily identifiable groups will help you target, measure and analyse the results of your calls.*
- *Different groups of customers will be available at varying times throughout the day.*
- *The more you know about the industries you are targeting and their practices the more informed you will be about the best times to call them.*
- *Be realistic about how many sales calls or sales visits you can make in one day.*
- *It is far better to make good qualified appointments than those just to make numbers up to reach targets.*
- *Before picking up the telephone to make your call or going out to the sales interview set your objective, be clear what you want to achieve from the sales interview.*
- *Remember: the higher the value of the purchase the longer it will take to get the sale.*
- *Research your prospective customer before calling on them.*
- *Before calling or visiting a prospective customer make sure you have all the necessary leaflets, price lists and brochures to hand. Prepare as well as you can before any sales interview.*

PART 2

THE SALES STRUCTURE

CHAPTER 6

The Sales Structure – Approach

Using a sales structure can help you keep your sales interview on course. The structure I am going to use is called **ADDIN** which stands for **Approach, Discussion, Diagnosis, Implications, Needs**. By using this I hope you will add in your product or service to the prospective customer's business, home or lifestyle. You can use this structure both on the telephone and the in face-to-face sales interview.

I will show you how, by using this structure, you can switch the prospective customer from the negative buying motivations to the positive buying motivations. This chapter examines the first stage of the telephone sales call and the face-to-face sales interview: Approach. There is also a handy summary of the telephone sales call and the sales visit structure later in this book.

THE APPROACH

The most obvious difference between telephone selling and face-to-face selling is that the telephone is a non-visual tool. In telephone selling the prospective customer will be judging you on how you sound and what you say. In face-to-face selling the prospective customer will be judging you, certainly initially, on your appearance, your voice and your body language. So making the right impression whether that is on the telephone or in person is vital.

There are also some other key differences in the two types of selling. In face-to-face selling:

- You have a longer period of time in which to make a sale.
- You are also forming an impression of the prospective customer by his voice, body language and appearance.
- You can gain more information about the organisation you are selling to by studying its surroundings
- You may come across more objections because the prospective customer has time to air these.
- In face-to-face selling you need to be personable and presentable.
- Personality will have more of an impact in face-to-face selling.

At the beginning of the telephone sales call or the face-to-face sales interview it is highly likely that you will experience the negative buying motivation from the prospective customers, ie ***'I don't trust you'***. You need to change this to the positive buying motivation, ie ***'I am important'***. So how do you do this?

> You need to reduce the relationship tension by building rapport and credibility.

On the telephone this means using your voice in the most appropriate way, that is by matching and mirroring the tone and pace of the prospective customer to make him feel comfortable.

In a face-to-face selling situation you can use both your voice and body language to establish and build rapport.

In addition, you should give early evidence of your competence by asking the right questions identifying with the prospective customer's business or personal needs, but more about this later.

THE TELEPHONE SALES CALL – APPROACH

Firstly you will need to introduce yourself. You should say your name and your company name clearly and slowly and also say briefly what your company does. Research has shown that in the first couple of seconds when someone lifts the receiver they are not listening but their mind is on what they were doing when the telephone rang. This is why we often forget the person's name and have to ask them to repeat it. So, give them time to tune into you.

TOP TIPS

Make your introduction as succinct as possible. For example, 'Good morning I'm John Smith from ABC Limited. We manufacture widgets for the electronics industry.'

Also remember to 'smile while you dial!' It might sound corny but by lifting your voice you inject more enthusiasm into it. It also helps to make you feel more confident because a smile will lift your body language and send positive messages to the brain.

TOP TIPS

Put the word SMILE in big letters in front of your telephone where you can see it. No one wants to talk to someone who sounds as if they're about to jump off a cliff and if you're not upbeat about your products or services then why should your prospective customer be?

ACTION POINT

Write down how you are going to introduce yourself, your company and a brief statement about what your company does.

Getting the name correct

You can make the prospective customer feel important by firstly addressing them by their correct name and title.

You need to judge this accurately. I know sales people who have lost the sale by being too familiar and addressing someone by their first name when they should have used the surname and their title.

EXAMPLE

I once overheard a conversation in an office where I was a visitor. The chairman's personal assistant received a telephone call from a sales person trying to sell her stationery. He immediately addressed her by her first name, which was 'Jane.' Her rather haughty reply was, 'Do I know you?' Needless to say the sales person, having got through to the correct person, blew the sale by being overfamiliar.

The simple rule in getting this right is to always err on the side of formality until invited to address them otherwise. It is good manners after all. You can also gauge how to respond by the way they introduce themselves to you. For example, if I were to introduce myself as Pauline Rowson, then it is acceptable for you to call me Pauline. If however I introduced myself as Mrs Pauline Rowson, or Mrs Rowson then I would expect to be addressed as Mrs Rowson. If in doubt ask. You can always say, 'Is it all right if I call you xxxx?'

You might also wish to take into consideration the person's age and their position in the organisation. If the prospective customer is older than you, or very senior in the organisation, then respect this by being more formal in the way you address them. You might also find some organisations are traditionally more formal in their approach than others.

TOP TIPS

Use the person's name in your conversation, particularly at the beginning of the sales interview. This is also a very useful technique for remembering someone's name.

Your voice

On the telephone you need to establish and build rapport very quickly. You do not have the same amount of time to win over your prospective customer as you would have face-to-face. One of the ways you can quickly establish rapport is by using your voice to maximum effect.

Volume of your voice

Don't shout and don't talk too quietly. If you shout down the line the hearer will be put off by too loud a voice. Conversely if you are too quiet they will walk all over you. The voice must convey a great deal. The first few seconds are vital for the right impression – warm, friendly, alert and wanting to communicate effectively.

Vary your pitch

Make sure you don't sound droll. The telephone drains 30% of the energy level in your voice, so make sure you lift it. Vary your pitch and pace to make it sound more interesting and enthusiastic.

It's not what you say it's the way that you say it!! Enthusiasm is infectious; inject it in your voice.

ACTION POINT

One way to improve the pitch and pace of your voice is to practise reading aloud, and especially to young children where you need to use different voices to engage and keep their interest.

Don't sound too nice!

If you are a woman with a high pitched voice or you talk in a little girl, breathless voice, then you might have problems being taken seriously. If your voice is too sugary you will also sound insincere.

ACTION POINT

Record yourself. Listen to how your voice sounds. If you need to make it sound more sincere, then try slowing down and keeping your body language and in particular your head still. This will inject more authority into your voice.

Accents

Ensure your prospective customer can understand what you are saying. There is nothing wrong in having an accent, most of us do, but it's no good if the prospective customer can't understand a thing you are saying. The telephone can exaggerate accents making them even more difficult to understand.

If you finish your sentences high, as if you are asking a question when you are actually stating a fact, this will make you sound as if you are continually seeking the other person's approval before proceeding with your speech. It can be irritating to the listener and is very common in some regional accents. Listen for it and try and correct it. Hearing it in others first may help you to hear it in your own patterns of speech.

ACTION POINT

Record yourself and listen to how you sound. Do you need to lower your tone of voice, speak more clearly or simply slow down when you talk? Check for the overuse of fillers, such as 'er', 'um', 'you know', plus those inflections in your voice which will weaken the power of what you are saying, and irritate your prospective customer. Develop an ear for them and reward yourself when you are improving. You may need the honest opinion of a colleague in order to find the areas that are difficult for others to understand.

Build rapport

You can build rapport with your prospective customer by mirroring/ pacing your voice with theirs. There is an old maxim, 'People buy people'. If the prospective customer likes the sound of you, and enjoys talking to you, then they are much more likely to buy from you. This does not mean to say that you are gushingly friendly, but that you should try and match the prospective customer's voice. For example, if they are slower speaking, then slow your own speech. If you don't and continue to talk at them like a babbling idiot, or fire questions at them, they will feel intimidated and won't listen. They will want to get you off the phone as quickly as possible. Likewise, if you are talking to a very direct individual, then be direct back. They will respect and respond to that.

Body posture

Look and be alert. If your body is slouched your voice will sound slouched. It will give the impression that you couldn't care less and no one is going to buy from you then. If you can't be bothered, why should they?

Imagine the other person sitting in front of you. How would you look then? Alert and interested I hope. Keep your head up. This puts less pressure on your vocal chords and will also save you from crooking the telephone under your chin and against your shoulder, which will lead to neck and back problems later.

Body language

Use the same body language on the telephone as you would normally face-to-face. This enables the enthusiasm in your voice to come through.

> **TOP TIPS**
> Stand up to take difficult calls; it gives your voice more authority.

THE FACE-TO-FACE SALES INTERVIEW – APPROACH

> **TOP TIPS**
> When visiting an individual in his home to make a sale, always ensure you arrive punctually. Many a sale is lost because the sales person failed to arrive on time.

When visiting an organisation in order to make a sale always ensure you arrive early. Sit (or better still, stand – it aids authority and gives you energy) in reception. Here you can glean a great deal about an organisation from your first visit. Consider the following: What do the premises look like? Are they falling to pieces? If so how healthy are that organisation's finances, and therefore its ability to pay you?

How well are you greeted? Is the receptionist friendly and welcoming or hostile? What does this tell you about the company?

Receptions are gossip zones. They shouldn't be but many businesses neglect this vital area. This is good news for the sales person because he can learn a great deal about the company from eavesdropping on the gossip. For example if the staff are moaning about redundancies then I would question the ability of the company to pay you unless you are there to help them with redundancies!

You might also learn something about the person you are going to visit.

EXAMPLE

I was visiting a large multinational organisation in Surrey. I was due to see the Commercial Director, in this instance to sell in my training services. The two women on reception decided to undertake a character assassination on the man I was visiting. I learnt a great deal about him in those few minutes, not all of it true I am sure, but it gave me some insight into the nature of the person I was about to visit and some clues on how to approach the interview! I'm happy to report that I won the contract.

While waiting in reception take a look at the literature lying around on the tables. Does the company have a press cuttings file, or a company newsletter? If so read it while waiting for your appointment, it could provide you with valuable information, which you may be able to refer to in your conversation with the prospective customer to demonstrate your interest in them. What awards are on display on the walls and what does this tell you about the company?

Also don't forget the Gatekeeper – the receptionist. Take time to be pleasant, and ask gentle questions about the business if you can, but don't pry too deeply. Keep the conversation light and friendly. And don't forget the receptionist could be related to the person you are visiting and therefore be an Influencer in that Decision Making Unit, so don't pass any comments you might later regret.

If the prospective customer is visiting you at your premises, or coming on to your exhibition stand, then examine the impression you and your organisation are giving out, and make sure it is the correct one.

FIRST IMPRESSIONS COUNT

You never get a second chance to make a first impression. With the face-to-face sales interview first impressions are vital. If you don't give out the correct impression then you could easily lose the sale at the first post.

> You begin to close the sale the first few seconds you meet the prospective customer.

When you meet someone they will sum you up in the first five seconds. They will be taking into consideration your appearance, your body language and the way you speak. A first impression can be a lasting impression, so take time to get it right.

Your appearance

Many people overlook this important aspect and while you can't possibly know the prospective customer's tastes in clothing and grooming you can eliminate some mistakes by following some very simple guidelines.

Make sure your shoes are clean and not shabby. Ensure that you are dressed smartly and conservatively rather than eccentrically, unless you happen to be visiting someone in one of the more creative industries where you might have more scope to assert your individual taste. I have been present at a number of sales presentations where someone has lost the sale because their shoes and general appearance do not meet the prospective customer's expectations.

When it comes to appearance for women there is an additional rule. The more flesh you show the less credible you will be. You need to look professional and competent, not as if you are about to go to the beach or nightclub.

TOP TIPS

Dress appropriately for the industry or person you are visiting.

Ask yourself: Where am I going? Who am I seeing? What do I wear?

If you dress too inappropriately you will alienate your prospect.

Grooming

Good grooming and hygiene is essential. Your hair should be clean and tidy with no tell-tale dandruff on your collar. Don't overdo the aftershave or perfume as this can cause some people to take an instant dislike to you. Also check your breath.

TOP TIPS

A good way to know if you suffer from bad breath is to lick the inside of your wrist, wait for five seconds then sniff it. This will tell you.

If this is a problem for you, visit a dentist and ask his professional advice. Having bad breath, like having bad body odour, is something even your best friends won't tell you. It is so personal and delicate and yet something can be done about both.

The group sales presentation

If you are giving a sales presentation to a group of people then you need to project authority. If you are a woman dress classic rather than too fussy. Darker suits aid authority and you can combine this with a striking necklace or scarf.

For both men and women check the fit of the suit when buttoned up. When presenting formally always stand and make sure your jacket is buttoned up.

YOUR BODY LANGUAGE

55% of the impression you give out is through your appearance and body language.

The way you greet your prospective customer will also create an impression.

TOP TIPS

Walk forwards with your arm outstretched, not too stiff but with your elbow tucked into your waist.

Always offer your hand first.

As you shake hands with the prospective customer smile at him and give him good eye contact.

Your handshake should be firm and dry.

It is not always easy to know if you are giving a good handshake, as people won't tell you. So, why not try this simple exercise.

ACTION POINT

Shake hands with someone you know and trust and ask them for their honest opinion.

The double clutch handshake, often referred to as the 'politician's handshake,' is where someone clasps your hand with both of theirs. It is a dominant gesture and can often be interpreted as being patronising, so avoid using it. To find out how you should react if someone uses this handshake on you read chapter 13.

Women should practise the 'man's handshake' this is where you take the whole hand and not just the fingertips. A good firm confident grip gives the impression you are confident (even if you're not.)

Sit down only when invited to do so. Keep your body language open and sit back in the chair. Try to avoid crossing your legs because although it might feel comfortable it can give the impression of being hostile or defensive. Do not put anything on the prospective customer's desk or table without asking first. The desk or table is their territory and you are invading their space and therefore being threatening unless you ask their permission first. A simple question such as, 'Is it OK if I use your desk?' or 'Is it all right if I put my presenter here?' will suffice. (I cover interpreting the prospective customer's body language and using body language effectively during the sales interview in chapter 9.)

SETTING THE TONE

Before getting into the sales interview in depth you need to set the tone. Begin by opening the conversation with neutral remarks. This can include comments on the traffic, the weather, their premises, or the awards displayed on the wall in reception. Different personalities need different tactics and I look at this in more detail in chapter 13.

Remember the positive buying motivations, the first one of which is **'I am important'.** You need to make the prospective customer feel important by:

- Complimenting him or his organisation
- Using his name early in the conversation
- Using positive body language which includes a good handshake and eye contact
- Asking permission before sitting or using his desk

At an exhibition

Before I move on to the next stage in our sales structure it is worth giving you a few additional tips on using the correct body language at an exhibition.

Don't sit on your stand and wait for people to come up to you; they won't. People are wary and reluctant to open conversations, so you need to do it. Give them good eye contact, smile and open the conversation gently, a neutral comment can be best.

Always start with an open question rather than a closed one, for example ask them 'how' they are enjoying the exhibition rather than 'are' they enjoying the exhibition.

Don't stand at the front of your exhibition unit with your arms folded – you will look like a police officer guarding the entrance and no one will approach you. And don't patrol the entrance to your stand either, walking up and down in front of it. Move out slightly into the aisle and be welcoming.

If you have something of interest on display on your stand this can help capture on-lookers and then you can start talking to them. The sales structure I use in this book (ADDIN) also applies to selling at an exhibition.

QUICK RECAP

- *On the telephone sales call make your introduction as succinct as possible.*
- *Smile while you dial! A smile lifts your voice and gives it more enthusiasm.*
- *Build rapport with your caller by matching the speed of their voice, vary your pitch and make sure you do not sound droll.*
- *If your body is slouched your voice will sound slouched.*
- *Use the same body language on the telephone as you would normally face-to-face.*
- *On the face-to-face sales interview arrive early for an appointment and see what you can glean about that organisation in reception.*
- *55% of the impression you make on other people is based on your appearance and your body language so take time to get this right.*
- *Your handshake should be firm and dry.*
- *Keep your body language open.*

CHAPTER 7

The Sales Structure – Discussion

Having introduced yourself and your company succinctly and clearly, and having built rapport with the prospective customer at the Approach stage (thereby satisfying the positive buying motivation 'I am important'), you now need to move on to the next stage of the sales structure ADDIN: Discussion. This chapter examines how you can stimulate and steer the discussion both on the telephone sales call and in the face-to-face sales interview and looks at the questioning techniques needed.

DISCUSSION

It is not enough to simply telephone a prospective customer and ask for an appointment to visit them. After all, why should they give up their precious time to talk to you? And in the face-to-face sales interview it is not enough to tell the prospective customer what you have on offer and expect them to buy. You need to demonstrate to the prospective customer that what you are offering fulfils a need they have, or can help solve a problem. In order to do this you need to ask the correct questions and probe their needs.

You want the prospective customer to open up and talk to you. You want to find out about their business and their needs, and only then can you sell in the corresponding benefit to match these needs.

One of the best ways of doing this, and thereby switching the prospective customer from the negative buying motivations: '*I don't trust you*', '*I don't need you*', to the positive ones: '*I am important*', '*Consider my needs*' is to get them talking and to do this you need to ask them open questions.

Asking open questions is a critical part of the sales interview.

Open questions

Open questions are those that cannot be answered with a simple yes or no. They begin with:

- Who
- What
- Why
- How
- When
- Where

Asking open questions will help you to:

- Properly understand what it is the prospective customer wants
- Make him feel important
- Find out how he feels about you and your organisation
- Control the conversation
- Understand his needs

Closed questions

If you ask closed questions which begin with: 'is/are', 'should/shall', 'will/would', 'could/can', 'did/do', you will make life a lot harder for yourself, particularly with an individual who is not naturally forthcoming, or who is hostile, because he can answer in a monosyllable, and you will not get the information you need.

For example, if I were to ask you: 'Did you go out last night?' You could simply answer, 'Yes.' Then I would need to ask 'Where did you go?' I have had to ask two questions. Whereas by using an open question I could simply have asked: 'Where did you go last night?' or 'What did you do last night?' Then I would have received from you information on your evening's activities.

I am not saying you should never use closed questions. They have their place. They can be used to obtain clarification or to elicit a specific response. Unfortunately as we grow older we lose the habit of asking open questions, and it is highly likely you will need to practise these to re-learn this lost art.

ACTION POINT

When you are at a social or a business function, set yourself a goal of finding someone you don't know and obtaining information from them by asking open questions. I guarantee they will be most impressed with you and you will probably have won a friend for life!

THE TELEPHONE SALES CALL – DISCUSSION

Remember that on the telephone you have less time to make an impact and to ask questions. The discussion phase, therefore, is shorter than in the face-to-face sales interview. On the telephone you need to engage the prospective customer's attention quickly. In order to do this you need to ask fewer open questions, three or four at the most. And you need to begin these by asking an **open attention question,** which is designed to get the prospective customer talking to you right at the beginning of the call.

Open attention questions

EXAMPLE

A contact lens manufacturer was making telephone sales calls to opticians with the objective of getting the opticians to stock the manufacturer's contact lenses. The opening attention question was: 'What percentage of your business is contact lens driven?' This question got the optician talking straight away and gave the telephone sales operator some valuable information.

Here is another example: a company manufacturing capital equipment for the printing and labelling industry asked its prospective customers: '*What* are your plans for investment in new equipment for the next 12 months?' And if you still haven't got the point, here is another example taken from a company selling chemicals to industry: '*What* chemicals do you currently use in your cleaning processes?'

Some people find it very difficult jumping straight in with what they see as a very direct question. This is because they have lost the art of asking an open question. They are also afraid that the prospect is going to say, 'What's it got to do with you?' or 'Mind your own business', but the majority of people don't – they simply answer the question. All right, so their voice might sound wary, (remember they might still be on the negative buying motivation of '*I don't trust you*') but you will get them talking and then you can go on to ask other open questions.

Following the open attention question you need to probe for further information to find out if the benefits of your products or services will fulfil a need. You will do this by asking **open situation questions**.

Open situation questions

> You need to ask open situation questions which are designed to probe the situation.

On the telephone sales call you will need to ask three or four open situation questions at the most. For example our contact lens manufacturer can ask:

- What type of contact lenses do you use?
- Which are the most popular ones?
- How many do you use in an average month?
- Who currently supplies you?

Our capital equipment manufacturer of machinery for the labelling and printing industry can ask:

- What type of equipment do you currently use?
- What type of labels do you produce?
- What width and colour range?
- Who typically are your customers?

ACTION POINT

If you are making telephone sales calls, think about your own business and your prospective customers. Now write down your open attention question and three or four open situation questions.

Keep your questions in front of you when making your calls.

THE FACE-TO-FACE SALES INTERVIEW – DISCUSSION

TOP TIPS

Don't hand your literature to a prospective customer at the beginning of the sale because this will guarantee he will not be listening to you, or wanting to participate in the discussion. Instead he will be flicking through your literature. Save your literature until the end of the sales process.

In the face-to-face sales interview there is no need to ask the open attention question because you already have their attention – the prospective customer is sitting in front of you. But you do need to ask good open questions and open situation questions. You also have much more time to ask these open situation questions. It is likely that the sales interview will take anything from 20 minutes to an hour, and sometimes possibly longer. So, if you do it correctly, you should gain a great deal of information from the prospective customer. Here are some further examples of open situation questions you could use.

EXAMPLE

A company selling luxury boats to individuals could ask:

- *How are you intending to use the boat?*
- *Where do you usually motor?*
- *What arrangements have you made to moor the boat?*
- *How many people does the boat need to accommodate?*

A company selling training courses could ask:

- *How many staff do you employ?*
- *What sort of markets do you operate in?*
- *Where do you currently export?*
- *How many people are you intending to train?*

- *What are their positions in your company?*
- *What are you hoping to achieve by the training?*
- *Where are you thinking of holding the training session?*

From all the above examples you will get information.

TOP TIPS

You cannot sell your product or service until you have information. Miss out this vital first stage and you will miss the sale!

The sales person who begins by launching into his sales spiel will fail. It is not enough to *tell* the prospective customer who you are and what you have to offer and then invite them to buy, the prospective customer needs to feel important, he needs to know that you have considered his needs, he also needs to see that your ideas will help him, ie the benefits of what you are offering will solve his problems or fulfil a need.

You might, however, find yourself under extreme pressure from your prospective customer who perhaps has given you an interview rather grudgingly. Here those negative buying motivations '*I don't trust you*', '*I don't need you*' will be predominant in the customer's mind. He will be highly sceptical and suspicious of you and your company. In this case he could very well start the sales interview by saying something like:

'So, come on then sell to me.'

Or

'I can only give you 10 minutes, what do you do?'

Or

'What are you going to sell me?'

Your instinct could be to launch into your sales spiel. Then having finished you sit back and say, 'So, are you interested?' to which the prospective customer replies, 'No thank you,' or 'I'll think about it.' Wrong! You have lost your chance of a potential sale. Curb that instinct; throw the ball back into the prospective customer's court.

EXAMPLE

A sales person is selling training courses to a director of a large organisation. The director is an impatient man who enjoys putting pressure on sales people who visit him.

Director: *'I can only give you 10 minutes, tell me what you do and how much it will cost me.'*
Sales person: *'I'd be delighted to tell you what we do, but first, so that I can find out how I can help you, I need to ask you a few questions. Tell me, what sort of training have you carried out in the past?'*
By asking an open situation question the sales person has improved his chances of making a sale.

TOP TIPS

Put pressure on the prospective customer to answer your questions.
Keep control of the interview at all times by using good questioning techniques, in particular open questions.
Remember it is your interview you should be driving it to a successful conclusion. Don't let the prospective customer hijack it.

Even if the prospective customer is reluctant to answer you to begin with, he will soon warm up once he gets talking about himself or his company. You will need to chip in with a few more open questions to keep the discussion going and from this you will be able to diagnose his needs. I cover this in the next chapter (p.79).

ACTION POINT

Write a list of the open situation questions you could use during a sales interview.

MORE QUESTIONING TECHNIQUES

Be careful about asking multiple questions. This is where you roll several questions into one. For example, 'How many people do you train Mr Jones and how often do you train them?' Which question is he likely to answer – the first or the last? Will you have got all the information you need? No.

TOP TIPS

Ask an open question, and wait for the answer. Resist the temptation to jump in and answer it for them, particularly if the prospective customer is a fairly slow individual and you are a rather quick and impatient one.

Also beware of using value-loaded questions. This is where you load your values on to the other person. For example, 'What do you think of these thick union reps?' You might get the answer, 'I am one.'

Leading questions can be used in some circumstances where you want to lead the prospective customer into giving a positive response but it can work against you, so you need to be careful. For example, if you say, 'You don't think this will work then?' you are likely to get the answer, 'No.' Leading questions can be used to close though, when asking for the business. For example, 'Shall I go ahead and place the order then?' Or 'You'll agree to present this idea to your directors then?' Hopefully they will say 'Yes.' There's more on closing in chapter 12.

Don't be afraid to ask who the company's current suppliers are; most people will tell you. But if they don't, then don't worry, you are more concerned with how they *feel* about their current suppliers than *who* they are – which brings me on to the next type of questions to ask to diagnose the need, which are covered in the following chapter.

QUICK RECAP

- *In order to switch the prospective customer from the negative buying motivations: 'I don't trust you', 'I don't need you' to the positive ones: 'I am important', 'Consider my needs' you need to get them talking by asking open questions.*
- *Open questions are those that cannot be answered with a simple yes or no. They begin with: 'who', 'what', 'why', 'how', 'when', 'where'.*
- *Closed questions, which begin with: 'is/are', 'will/would', 'could/can', 'should/shall', 'did/do' can be used to obtain clarification or to elicit a specific response.*
- *The discussion phase of the telephone sales interview is shorter than in the face-to-face sales interview.*
- *On the telephone you need to engage the prospective customer's attention quickly by asking fewer open questions and by starting with an open attention question.*
- *Open situation questions are designed to probe the situation.*
- *Keep your questions in front of you when making your telephone calls.*
- *You cannot sell your product or service until you have information. Miss out this vital first stage and you will miss the sale!*
- *Keep control of the interview at all times by using good questioning techniques, in particular open questions.*
- *Don't hand your literature to a prospective customer at the beginning of the sale, save it until the end of the sales process.*
- *Be careful about asking multiple questions and value-loaded questions.*
- *Leading questions can be used in some circumstances where you want to lead the prospective customer into giving a positive response and to close the sales interview.*

CHAPTER 8

The Sales Structure – Diagnosis, Implications and Needs

So you've got the prospective customer talking, you now need to be able to diagnose what his need is from the answers you have been given to your open questions. Following this you need to spell out the implications of his problem, and then show him how what you offer can help solve his problem or fulfil that need. This chapter examines how you do this. It covers the remaining stages of the ADDIN sales structure: Diagnosis, Implications and Needs, and shows you how to present the benefits of your products or services to the prospective customer.

DIAGNOSIS

Following on from the answers given to the open situation questions you've asked during the first stage of the sales interview you will need to ask some problem or needs questions. These will help you to probe the needs and problems of the prospective customer in order for you to be able to present your features and benefits to help satisfy those needs or solve the problems.

Problem or needs questions

Let's follow through on one of the previous examples I've used, that of the contact lens manufacturer:

Open attention question:
'*What* percentage of your business is contact lens driven?'

Open situation questions:
'What type of contact lenses do you use?'
'Which are the most popular ones?'
'How many do you use in an average month?'
'Who currently supplies you?'

Problem or needs questions:
'How satisfied are you with your current suppliers?'

Other problem or needs question examples can include:
'How satisfied are you with the quality of your current labels?'
'How often does the equipment let you down?'
'What sort of difficulties did that incur for your company?'
'How does this compare to your previous experiences?'

You might have noticed that most of the above questions are again open questions beginning with the words: 'who', 'what', and 'how', only 'which' isn't on the list of open questions but is an alternative question, where the prospective customer needs to express an opinion or make a choice.

ACTION POINT

Identify some problem or needs questions that you could ask your prospective customers.

Probing

You should also probe deeper following on from a needs or problem question.

EXAMPLE:

Sales person: *'How satisfied are you with your current suppliers?'*
Prospective customer: *'Fairly satisfied.'*
Sales person: *'Fairly? Why is that?' (Probing open question)*
Prospective customer: 'Well they don't always deliver when they say they will.'

By probing that bit deeper in this example the sales person has uncovered a problem on the part of the customer's current suppliers.

You can use comparative questions to help you with the probing stage. This is a variation on the theme of open questions but comparative questions can give you yet more information and can help you explore different angles.

For example:
'How does this compare with the previous/current model?'
'How do these proposals compare to those outlined in your letter?'

These questions can often be followed up by yet more open probing questions.

EXAMPLE

Sales person: *'How do our prices compare to what you are currently paying?'*
Comparative question

Prospective customer: *'Very favourably indeed.'*
Sales person: 'How?'
Probing open question

Prospective customer: *'Well, although you are dearer I am not getting the level of service from my current suppliers that I would like.'*
Sales person: *'And this high level of service is important to you?'*
Leading question

Prospective customer: *'Yes.'*
Sales person: *'Why is that particularly?'*
Open probing question

Prospective customer: *'Because we need our suppliers to respond to us quickly. We can't afford to have the computer system down because that affects our performance and we lose sales as a result.'*

From this discussion the sales person can diagnose that the prospective customer needs a high level of service, a rapid response and is prepared to pay a little more to be guaranteed this.

ACTION POINT

Can you identify some comparative questions that you could ask during the sales interview?

IMPLICATIONS AND NEEDS

The prospective customer in the above example has also stated the implications of his problem – that he will lose business if his computer system stays down for too long.

Now you can spell out the implications of the problems or needs you have uncovered from the prospective customer. Here you can fulfil the third stage of the positive buying motivations: '*Will your ideas help me?*'

For example: 'So, because your suppliers don't always deliver on time that must cause a delay for your customers.' Here you want the customer to agree with the implications by saying, 'Yes.' From the implications you can then go on to tell the prospective customer what he **needs** and how you can help to **fulfil** that need: 'So what you **need** is a next day guaranteed delivery on all orders no matter how small?'

Here is another example: 'So what you **need** then, Mr Jones, is a machine that is 99% efficient and reliable, that won't let you down and cause a problem with your customers?' What you are hoping is that Mr Jones will agree with your summary of his needs by saying 'Yes!'

You should then tell him how you can deliver this by selling in the appropriate feature and benefit that satisfies that need. For example: 'Our new ES123 Series will not only produce your two colour labels to excellent quality but also has a guaranteed non-failure rate.'

SUMMARISING OR REFLECTING

You can also use another technique in the sales process, that of summarising or reflecting, as it is sometimes called. This helps the prospective customer to see that you have listened to him and that you have correctly interpreted and understood his situation.

EXAMPLE

Sale sperson: *'So what you* **need** *is a rapid response to any queries or problems you have and if the system goes down a back-up will be in place, which will minimise down time.'*
Summarising skills – to show you have understood the implications of his problems and understood his needs
Prospective customer: *'Yes.'*
Sales person: *'Because we provide a 24 hour service we can give you round the clock support and back-up, thereby minimising any downtime and ensuring you don't lose sales. What's more we can also guarantee an engineer will be with you within two hours.'*
Here the sales person has sold in the relevant feature and benefit and has strengthened it with a further benefit

Don't oversell. Don't go into reams of features and benefits. This will only put them off. Give the features and benefits that are relevant and of interest to the prospective customer.

I have now completed the sales structure of ADDIN but I haven't quite finished the sales interview. There are a further three stages in the positive buying motivations before we can come away with the order. These are:

- What are the details?
- What are the problems?
- I approve.

WHAT ARE THE DETAILS?

After presenting the benefits of your products or services to the prospective customer to help him fulfil his need or solve his problem he may well come back to you with further questions.

Questions are a buying signal – welcome them. Answer them honestly and openly. Don't overpromise in order to get the sale because your customer will be disappointed when you can't deliver and you won't win any future business from him. Questions can come through at any time of the sales interview and not just at the end.

Sometimes you will need to answer questions as they arise, other times you might not be in the correct position to answer them, or would be wise to refrain from answering them at that particular point of the sales interview because you do not have all the information you need. The great danger is that if you respond to the prospective customer's question by answering it, then letting the prospective customer ask another question, in the end you are responding to his questions and he is in control of the interview. I have seen this happen countless times.

TOP TIPS

You need to stay in control of the sales interview and if you feel you are losing it then ask the prospective customer an open question to regain control.

After presenting the benefits of your products or services to the prospective customer to help him fulfil his need or solve his problem he may well come back to you with further questions.

This shows an interest in what you have to offer. Answer these questions honestly and accurately, and strengthen the sale by presenting additional benefits of your products or services, demonstrating how they can help the prospective customer. You can provide evidence of the value that you offer by quoting or showing testimonials from satisfied customers. You can also strengthen the sale by differentiating yourself from the competition.

In addition, you might find yourself in the position of discussing the finer details of the sale and suddenly under pressure to negotiate on certain aspects.

Some of the factors you can negotiate on can include:

- Price
  (Don't succumb to the temptation to reduce your prices as soon as the prospective customer puts pressure on you; it lowers what you have to offer. Restate the value of the product and stress its benefits to the customer.)
- Credit terms
- Delivery
- Quality of product
- Standardisation with purchaser's existing plant/system
- Design and technical merit of the product
- After sales service

Here are some tips to help you negotiate more successfully:

- Never give a concession. Trade it reluctantly. When people agree too quickly, both parties each feel they could have got a better deal and this can sour the relationship and the transaction. Leave the prospective customer feeling he's done a good deal too.
- Always appear reasonable.
- Be courteous, don't rush the other side.
- Appear relaxed.
- Listen carefully and watch the body language for both positive and negative signs.

> Questions are a buying signal –welcome them. Answer them honestly and openly. Don't overpromise in order to get the sale because your customer will be disappointed when you can't deliver and you won't win any future business from him.

Acknowledge the question, and then ask an open question if you need more information. Resist the temptation to be drawn into giving an answer if you do not have all the information you need.

EXAMPLE

A marketing consultant is trying to win a new client.

Prospective customer: *'So how much do you charge then?'*
Sales person: *'Charges vary depending on what you would like help with, how much help you'd like and what is needed to meet your objectives. You mentioned earlier that you're particularly keen to raise your online profile. Who do you see as your key target audience here?'*

In this example the marketing consultant has partially answered the question and then thrown the ball back in the prospective customer's court by asking him an open question to get more information on the background to the brief.

Alternatively he could have said: 'I'll explain how the charges work in a moment, but first I need more information so that I can see how I can help you. Who do you see as your key target audience?'

WHAT ARE THE PROBLEMS?

These are objections that the prospective customer might raise. I go on to fully cover how to handle objections in chapter 11. However, as with questions, objections can be buying signals, particularly if you have handled the sales interview correctly.. Be encouraged that you are only one step away from winning the business, the '*I approve*' stage of the positive buying motivations.

I APPROVE

This stage is the final one in the sales interview and the one where you hopefully take the order, and get the sale. I look at how you do this and examine closing techniques in chapter 12.

QUICK RECAP

- *Use problem or need questions to identify areas of need and problems.*
- *Once you have the information you can then introduce the appropriate benefit that will help to solve the prospective customer's problems or satisfy the needs you have uncovered.*
- *Comparative questions can give you more information and can help you explore different angles.*
- *Summarising skills enable the prospective customer to see that you have listened and correctly understood the situation.*
- *Don't oversell. Give only the features and benefits that are relevant and of interest to the prospective customer.*
- *Questions are a buying signal – welcome them. Answer them honestly and openly.*
- *Acknowledge the question and then ask an open question if you need more information.*

CHAPTER 9

Body language

Before I look at objection handling and closing the sale there are two important areas of the sales interview that I need to cover; body language and listening skills. This chapter looks at body language and the following chapter examines listening skills.

Body language is a critical part of the face-to-face selling process. Your body language can create an impression and communicate a message to the prospective customer. Equally you can read what your prospective customers are thinking and feeling throughout the sales interview by studying their body language signals. Being aware of body language, using and interpreting it therefore is an important skill required by the sales person. This chapter looks at interpreting body language signals and examining your own to make sure you are giving out the correct signals.

BODY LANGUAGE

Some people are very good at disguising their body language; others tend to wear their heart on their sleeve. Their emotions are quite clearly visible through their expressions and by how they stand or shift position.

In order to be a successful sales person you need to develop an awareness of how you use your body language and whether or not you have any annoying mannerisms that could be giving out the wrong signals to a prospective customer.

ACTION POINT

Video a role play of a sales interview with a colleague. Play it back and examine your body language. Are there any nervous mannerisms or annoying habits that you need to curb, for example: sniffing, rubbing your nose or touching your face, shifting in your chair or fidgeting? You might identify further negative body language signals after reading this chapter.

As a sales person you also need to understand the body language signals you are receiving. You need to be able to look for and interpret them while at the same time driving the sales interview to a successful close. In addition, you need to be able to distinguish what is a body language signal from a nervous habit on the part of the prospective customer.

When reading body language you need to look at the whole person and the complete picture.

Just because someone has his arms crossed it does not necessarily mean he is hostile – it may just be his customary pose. If his arms and legs are crossed, and he is perhaps scowling or keeping his distance by sitting back in his seat, then the complete picture tells you this person is aggressive or hostile and is not going to co-operate.

Below I have listed some of the more common body language signals and their interpretation but you need to remember that different nationalities have different body language signs. If you are selling internationally, or to different cultures within your own community, you need to be aware of what these body language signals are.

DISTANCE – PERSONAL BODY SPACE

Personal space is the distance you feel comfortable with when meeting or reacting with another person. It varies from country to country, between individuals and genders, and in different situations. For example, the Italians and French have a much closer personal space distance and are more tactile than the British or Germans. The Japanese and Chinese also have closer body space zones and in India the personal space zone is practically non-existent.

In Britain the personal space distance is about three feet hence the old saying, 'Keep them at arm's length,' which is approximately three feet. This is why we often feel uncomfortable when someone sits next to us on a bus or train, or at a seminar. It is why we put our bags or briefcases on the seat beside us; we are creating and establishing our own personal space. In crowded places like trains or the underground tube in rush hour, or a crowded lift, it is not possible to have the personal space we like around us. In these situations people will often not look at one another but will look at the ceiling or the floor, and/or they will angle their body away from the other person. Where this is not always possible you will find that we keep our body language movements down to a minimum, keeping very still.

TOP TIPS

Don't loom in at people across their desk or get too close when you greet them or you will be invading their personal space and antagonising them.

BODY MOVEMENTS

Watch for movements in the prospective customer's body language. For example, do they lean forward when you say something? If so that shows interest in what you have just said. If they sit back, fold their arms or rub their ear that means they don't much like what you are saying. Be attuned to this, find out what it is they don't like or are uneasy about by asking them an open question.

Rubbing the eyes can mean the person doesn't like what they see, equally it could mean they are tired, or have something in their eye. You need to look at the other body language signals that accompany it. For example, has the person shifted position and moved away from you? Or have you just shown them a brochure or catalogue or given a demonstration of a piece of equipment and perhaps they are not keen on what they are seeing?

People who put their hand over their mouth when speaking are often said to be lying, but this can also be a habit with some individuals. Again, if someone covers their mouth when they are speaking look for any movements in body posture, any shifting of position and dropping of eye contact. If you get all three the prospective customer is probably not telling the whole truth.

Rubbing the neck can often mean someone is tired, but it can also mean the individual is embarrassed about something. Again, look for other body language signals which might accompany this gesture. Shifting position and rubbing the neck could be telling you that the prospective customer feels uncomfortable with you, your manner or what you are saying.

FACIAL EXPRESSIONS

This can speak volumes. Frowning, looking puzzled, surprised, interested, and bored. There is no secret to reading this body language except the ability to train yourself to look for it and recognise it when you see it.

TOP TIPS

Be careful not to give away your own feelings and convey the wrong impression through using negative facial expressions. Look interested and alert.

EYE CONTACT

Make sure you give good eye contact. Shifting or skittering eye contact can make you appear shifty and uneasy. Hard, concentrated eye contact can be construed as aggressive. Keep your eye contact on the eyes and forehead of the person who is speaking. Occasionally look away and then use direct eye contact to make a point, for example when you have something serious to say.

Maintain good eye contact with your prospective customer throughout the sales interview.

If your prospective customer isn't looking at you that could be because he is either at the negative buying motivation stages of '*I don't trust you*', '*I don't need you*', or he could be nervous, shy or arrogant. Your job is to win his eye contact and when you do to lock into it but not with hostility. If he looks away then you can do the same before trying to win it back again. And watch for when you do win eye contact. It could mean that you have just said something of interest to the prospective customer.

EXAMPLE

I remember pitching to a group of partners in a legal firm to win them as a marketing client. There were about 15 people seated around a boardroom table. At that stage I didn't know who the main decision maker was. I couldn't assume it was the senior partner as he might not have been the decision maker, or the key Influencer.

Whilst I was giving my presentation I was receiving some smiles and nods from a few friendly faces. The danger is to play to these friendly souls rather than to those not looking at you. One man in particular was busy writing, sitting well away from the table and not giving me any eye contact. His body language was telling me he was superior to the proceedings and that he didn't think he needed my help. He was very much in the first stages of the negative buying motivations: 'I don't need you'.

By his superior, non-participatory body language I judged him to be the main decision maker. I needed to get and keep his attention if I was to win the contract. Halfway through my presentation I started talking about the image of a legal firm being extremely important. At this his head came up and he gave me eye contract.

I discarded the rest of my presentation and focused solely on talking about image. He had given me a clear buying signal through his body language. I asked a couple of questions, he started answering them and yes, I won the contract.

If there is more than one person present during the sales interview don't be tempted to concentrate on only the main decision maker or who you think is the decision maker. Be attuned to the others, these could very well be Influencers. Include them in your conversation by giving them occasional eye contact and a smile, and by angling your body towards them. Depending on their role in the selling process you might of course need to ask them questions, and answer their questions, which gives you ample opportunity to bestow friendly and open body language signals in their direction. If you completely ignore them then you might find yourself losing the sale.

BODY POSTURE

Avoid giving out defensive gestures (although you may be on the receiving end of them), ie closed body language. This means crossed legs, crossed arms and sitting well back and stiffly in your seat.

If your prospective customer is using this defensive or hostile body posture then ask open questions to get him talking about himself or his business, then watch for a change in body language. When it begins to unfold and relax you know you're doing the job well and he is beginning to thaw and move into the more positive buying motivations; eg '*I am important*', '*Consider my needs*'.

Sitting down with hands and arms clasped behind the back of the neck is a superior body language gesture and can exhibit extreme confidence sometimes bordering on arrogance. It can also be accompanied by the chin held high. It is predominantly a male body language position, although competitive and dominant women will adopt this stance. This is one body language signal you should not mirror because it will threaten the other person's dominant position and in the selling situation you do not want to appear superior or aggressive to the prospective customer. In addition, make sure you yourself do not use this body language when on a sales interview.

Impressive signals

- Sit upright and alert.
- Sit forward to convey real interest.
- Keep your eyes on the speaker.

- If you need to take notes always ask if you can first. Don't take too many, as you will lose eye contact with the prospective customer. Just jot down key points.
- Turn your body to the prospective customer but not head on, angle it so that it is less confrontational especially if the interview is taking place across a desk or table.
- When listening, keep your body language open, no folded arms. If you have to cross your legs just cross at the ankles.

Things to avoid

Don't:

- Slouch
- Look down at notes, out of window, at the ceiling
- Doodle
- Physically turn away
- Fold your arms tightly across your body which says you're not listening
- Growl, frown, or use cynical expressions
- Fidget, play with your hair, tap a pen or jiggle your leg

ACTION POINT

To help you become more aware of body language, subtly watch people when out in a café or restaurant, or at a social or business function. Obviously don't stare or intrude, simply try and interpret the body language signals you are seeing.

BUILDING RAPPORT

It is important to build rapport with the prospective customer not just at the beginning of the sales interview but throughout the interview. When two people are getting along well they will naturally mirror each other's body language. You can use this technique in the sales interview.

Try to gently mirror the prospective customer's body language. Not in an obvious way but subtly. When the prospective customer moves forward in his seat, you move forward. When they move back, gently ease back yourself.

> Continually be aware of your own body language and do not give out negative signals. Be attuned to the prospective customer's body language.

QUICK RECAP

- *Body language can be used to create an impression, you can read what the other person is thinking and feeling through the use of their body language.*
- *You need to be aware of your own body language and be able to interpret the use of the prospective customer's body language.*
- *You can also use body language to build rapport with the prospective customer.*
- *Personal distance varies from country to country, don't invade the prospective customer's personal space.*
- *If the prospective customer leans forward when you say something it shows interest. This is a buying signal, capitalise on it by strengthening your benefit and asking open questions.*
- *If the prospective customer sits back, folds his arms or rubs his ears that means he doesn't much like what you are saying, ask an open question to get him talking or to find out why he isn't keen on what you are saying.*
- *Avoid defensive gestures, ie closed body language. This means crossed legs, crossed arms and sitting well back and stiffly in your seat.*
- *Maintain good eye contact with your prospective customer throughout the sales interview.*
- *If you need to take notes always ask if you can first. Don't take too many, as you will lose eye contact with the prospective customer.*
- *You can also build rapport by subtly mirroring the prospective customer's body language.*

CHAPTER 10

Listening skills

You can have the best sales structure in the world but it won't work unless you have good listening skills. Only by listening to the prospective customer will you know which areas of need to probe and therefore which questions to ask. This chapter examines how to improve your listening skills.

LISTENING

Listening well is vitally important in the sales structure. If you don't listen then you could lose out on critical information that can help you sell in the relevant feature and benefit. Listening skills are even more important on the telephone sales call because you do not have the body language signals that can tell you how a prospective customer feels about what you are saying.

Listening, really listening, is the hardest thing to do and the highest form of courtesy!

Try this quick questionnaire to find out how much you know about listening.

ACTION POINT

Answer either true or false to the following questions.

1. Most people listen more than they speak.
2. Good listeners don't say anything while they listen.
3. Good listeners look at the speaker.
4. People listen well when they feel strongly about the topic.
5. Listeners are more influenced by what is said than how it is said.
6. People listen to criticism.

Now examine the answers to see how many you got right.

1. Most people listen more than they speak.
True:
Yes, there are more people who listen more than they speak, yet we all know those individuals who like the sound of their own voice and who never give anyone else a chance of having their say.

There is a saying in selling – you have two ears and one mouth. You should be listening twice as much as you are talking. In addition, your listening needs to be of a high quality. By that I mean *really* listening, not simply letting something drift in one ear and out of the other.

When dealing with the prospective customer on the face-to face sales interview you need to be fully attuned to what he is saying, not only listening but putting it together with the body language signals you are receiving to interpret the real meaning behind the words.

TOP TIPS

The good sales person listens to the prospective customer.

2. Good listeners don't say anything while they listen.

False:

Good listeners, while not actually speaking will make the 'listening noises' when they listen, eg 'uh huh,' 'I see,' 'Really.' This helps to confirm to the prospective customer that you are genuinely listening. This is particularly important when dealing with the telephone sales call as it will help you to build rapport. It is also vital in the face-to-face selling situation where you can also use your body language to show that you are listening.

For example:

- Sitting forward in your seat
- Looking at the speaker
- Angling your head on one side
- Looking interested

3. Good listeners look at the speaker.

True:

Good listeners *always* look at the speaker, it is the simplest way to show that you are truly listening. Have you ever been on the end of a conversation where the person listening looks away, or beyond you? Or with someone who asks you a question and then looks away just as you answer it? How did you feel? Pretty cross and upset I should imagine. When looking at the speaker keep your expression open, interested and concerned, this way you are signalling to them that they have your full attention.

4. People listen well when they feel strongly about the topic.

False:

People do not listen well when they feel strongly about a topic because their own feelings get in the way. They are just waiting for the speaker to finish so they can jump in and give their views.

Think about a conversation you've had in the past, with a friend or colleague when discussing something that you have strong views about – how quickly did you jump in with your opinion? Was it before they even finished speaking? When the other person was speaking were you really listening or was your mind racing to put forward your experience or views?

TOP TIPS

If you feel you want to interrupt the prospective customer, think about pausing and breathing before you do. A pause before you speak can also add significance.

5. Listeners are more influenced by what is said than how it is said.

True:

Think about the great speakers, or those personalities on television whom you find persuasive. It is not so much the actual words they are speaking but the way they say them that influences you. If they used the same words but put no meaning, passion or enthusiasm into them then you would soon become bored and stop listening.

As a sales person, having passion for what you are selling will show through in your voice and will encourage your prospective customer to listen and believe in what you have to offer.

If your prospective customer doesn't have much passion in his voice, and is rather a dull speaker, then you will need all your powers of concentration to continue to listen to him. Don't judge him by the way he speaks but listen to the content of the speech and watch for body language signals.

6. People listen to criticism.

False:

We do not listen well to criticism because our personal feelings get in the way. While we are being criticised or blamed we are often thinking, 'how dare they?' We become upset and indignant. We all think our own view is the real one. It is not. This can happen when the prospective customer raises an objection. He might be criticising something your company has done, and instead of listening to what he is saying you have gone on the defensive and your mind is racing to refute the criticism. I examine how to handle objections in chapter 11.

Whether it is an objection or a question the prospective customer is asking, listen intently and do not think ahead.

TWO TYPES OF LISTENING

As more and more of our communication becomes visual, ie internet and text based, we are forgetting how to listen. Listening involves both the ability to understand what is being said, and the ability to organise and analyse the messages in order to retain them for subsequent use.

There are two types of listening:

1. Casual listening
2. Critical listening

Casual listening

Casual listening is what we tend to do most of the time. We are only half listening, we retain bits of the conversation and we discard other parts of it. As a result you often get the following scenario between two people:

'Don't forget you're seeing Mr Smith today at 11am.'

'Am I? You didn't tell me that.'

'I told you two days ago. You weren't listening.'

Critical listening

Critical listening requires concentration and stamina. It is what is required in a selling situation and what a good sales person will practise. Here you are listening to the prospective customer, retaining what he says, storing it away and then retrieving some of it later when you need it.

What stops us listening?

There are many things that prevent us from listening, not least of which is laziness. We simply can't be bothered. Or maybe we've never been trained to listen. Perhaps our upbringing is such that no one has listened to us so why should we listen to them?

Here are some of the things that prevent us from listening:

Physical tiredness or discomfort

We may be tired or hungry. We may be hot or cold. We may be under stress and feel anxious or unwell.

If you are cramming too many sales visits into one day, or travelling too far this could easily show in your manner and affect your ability to listen. In addition, you may have been caught in a traffic jam, or your journey to the prospective customer taken longer than expected, and you arrive desperate to go to the lavatory. It may seem pretty basic to say it but do make sure you are comfortable during the sales interview otherwise your discomfort *will* stop you from listening.

Distractions and mind wandering

We may be distracted because of a noise. Or we may be thinking ahead of all the things that need to be done. We may be worried about someone or something.

On the telephone sales call, because the prospective customer can't see you, you can be tempted to do other things while listening to him. This means you won't be fully concentrating and you could miss out on vital information.

TOP TIPS

Give the telephone call and the prospective customer your full attention. Move away from your desk, computer screen or whatever distracts you if you can. Imagine the prospective customer is in front of you and behave accordingly. It will show through in your voice and improve your powers of listening.

Reactions to the speaker

We may dislike the person who is talking to us. We may find him boring or opinionated.

On the telephone sales call we might form an opinion of the prospective customer by his voice that triggers this view. Just because the prospective customer talks in a gruff, abrupt manner it does not necessarily mean he is rude. You must keep an open mind and judge the content of what he is saying and listen to the words he is using rather than the way he speaks.

Preconceived ideas

We may have preconceived ideas about the person we are communicating with because we have been told something about them. Perhaps we have been told that this particular prospective customer is going to be awkward and difficult. This will influence how we then handle him.

For example: a buyer in a large corporation has a reputation for being tough. You've been told by nearly everyone in the office that he is abrupt and rude, and extremely difficult to deal with. If you allow this to colour your view of that person then you could go into the sales interview aggressively, thinking, 'He's not going to get the better of me.' This will show in your body language and come through in your voice. The prospective customer will pick this up and act aggressively in return. You will NOT win the sale.

Alternatively if you go into the sales interview quaking in your shoes, thinking you haven't got a chance of getting the business, then you will behave submissively. Your body language will be defensive and you will allow the prospective customer to dominate you. You will NOT win the sale.

You need to clear your mind of what you've been told and get a good, healthy inner dialogue. Something along the lines of, 'I will form my own impression based on what I hear, learn and see of the customer.' 'I believe I can genuinely help him and his business.'

If you go into the sales interview with an open mind, prepared to listen then often the 'difficult person' is no trouble at all. And you will come away with the business.

Strong emotions and prejudices

We inherit prejudices and beliefs from our parents, guardians, teachers, religious leaders, friends and many others. Perhaps we have been 'conditioned' not to like or understand people who are from a different culture? Perhaps we have been 'conditioned' to believe we are superior to others because of our education or social standing. Or we may be prejudiced towards someone because of his or her gender or his or her size. If this is so then we take those prejudices with us when we meet someone face-to-face and these prejudices can influence the whole exchange between you and that person, and, as a result, you may be patronising or hostile towards them.

It is hard to clear your mind of prejudices before meeting someone because instinctively we try and 'place' people in order to give us a framework for reacting with them, but that framework can be very wonky to begin with.

> The good sales person does not judge anyone but keeps an open mind.

Different perspectives

We see things differently to the person talking and we disagree with them. This will influence the whole way we react with them.

Desire to talk

Many of us love to talk most of the time, to be the centre of attention; we love the sound of our own voice and think that only our opinions really count. This prevents us from listening. To be a good listener, and hence a good sales person, we must cease to be self-absorbed and be genuinely interested in the other person. If you find that during the sales interview you are doing more talking than the prospective customer then you are losing it.

ACTION POINT

Take five minutes a day to sit quietly somewhere, close your eyes and listen to all the sounds around you. Become conscious of them. How many different sounds can you hear? In addition to improving your listening skills this can also be relaxing.

Listen to the radio as much as possible, talk programmes, not music. What information did you receive? Can you summarise it? This will also help you to improve your summarising skills which I mentioned in chapter 8.

TOP TIPS

To improve listening skills

- Start listening with the first word and then listen intently
- Turn off all negative thoughts you have about the person speaking
- Think at the speed they're talking, don't jump ahead
- Do not interrupt
- Judge the content and not the delivery
- Suspend your judgement and keep an open mind
- Resist distractions if you possibly can
- Ask questions once they have finished talking to probe their feelings, reactions, or get more details
- Use positive body language. Lean towards them
- Use good eye contact.

RECOGNISING THE DIFFERENT TYPES OF LISTENER

There are many different types of listeners. You or your prospective customer might be one of the following. As you read through the descriptions below think of your own behaviour, and see if you can identify yourself.

The Self Centred Listener

This person spends so much time thinking about themselves that they cannot wait for a pause in the conversation to interject their views forcibly. They speak 90% of the time in any conversation and see talking as a way of gaining power and respect from others.

The Know Alls

These give the impression that they have superior experience on most topics and consequently listen to only 20% of what has been said. They are quick with instant potted solutions to most problems and cannot wait to point out a better personal experience. They appear inattentive, expressionless, sometimes bored.

The Aggressive Listeners

These listeners try so hard to be good listeners that they intimidate people with their staring eyes and intensive behaviour.

The Repeaters

This type of listener repeats your words immediately afterwards. They have a habit of finishing off your sentences for you. This can often be interpreted as a sign of nervousness or lack of self confidence.

The Fidgeters

Fidgeters are continually moving their heads looking for eye contact and other more interesting people or happenings elsewhere.

Readily Agreeable Listeners

These people agree too readily with everything you say. They nod while you are speaking and are afraid to be controversial and run the risk of annoying you. This is often a sign of submissive behaviour. It can leave the sales person very confused about how the prospective customer really feels.

Inaccurate listeners

Inaccurate listeners pick up certain emotive words and jump to conclusions accordingly. They often appear bigoted in their opinions. They are so pre-occupied with their own self interests and everyday work pressures that they are not prepared to make time for really listening.

> Are you one of these listeners? I hope not because of none of these make good sales people!

QUICK RECAP

- *Listening is an essential part of being a good sales person.*
- *The good sales person listens to the prospective customer. There is a saying – you have two ears and one mouth. You should be listening twice as much as you are talking.*
- *Listening involves:*
  - *the ability to understand what is being said.*
  - *the ability to organise and analyse the messages in order to retain them for subsequent use.*
- *There are two types of listening: casual listening and critical listening.*
- *There are many reasons why we don't listen properly: physical tiredness or discomfort, desire to talk, different perspectives, strong emotions and prejudices, preconceived ideas, reactions to the speaker and simple distractions and mind wandering.*
- *It takes practice and concentration to listen properly.*
- *The good sales person does not judge anyone but keeps an open mind.*

CHAPTER 11

Handling objections

Objections can come at any time throughout the sales interview. You need to be prepared to handle them. Many sales people are afraid of objections but instead you should welcome them because they can show interest. There is a correct way of dealing with objections and this chapter looks at the techniques for successfully handling them.

OBJECTION HANDLING

In order to handle objections in a professional manner you need to:

- Be prepared for them
- Listen to them
- Don't take them personally, welcome them, they show interest
- Ask open questions to probe the objection.
- Answer the objection by giving your compensating benefit
- Be sincere and honest

I will examine these points in more detail later in this chapter. First though let's see where objections fit into the positive buying motivations process.

Positive buying motivations

I am important

Approach:

Build and establish rapport, use the prospective customer's name, open the conversation.

↓

Consider my needs

Discussion:

Ask open questions, listen actively, probe to find the need or problem.

↓

Will your ideas help me?

Diagnosis:

Present the features and benefits that will help to meet the prospective customer's needs and/or solve his problems.

↓

What are the details?

Implications and Needs:

Answer the prospective customer's questions, listen to his concerns. Close the sale and ask for the business if possible.

↓

What are the snags?
Objections:
Handle outstanding objections.
↓
I approve
Close:
Close the sale and take the order.

So now you can see how far down the buying motivation process objections come. You are one step away from getting the business. If you handle the objections correctly, professionally and genuinely then you have every chance of winning the business.

However, objections don't always come at the end of the sales interview but can arise at any time. For example, an objection might come while you are still at the *discussion stage* when you haven't got enough information about the prospective customer, his needs or his problems to adequately answer it. Here, you will need to acknowledge the objection and regain control of the interview by asking another open question.

EXAMPLE

Prospective customer: *'But I can't afford to change suppliers at the moment.'*
Objection

Sales person: *'What do you mean?'*
Open question

Prospective customer: *'Well I have an agreement with another supplier which ties me in for another year.'*
Prospective customer elaborates the objection – giving you more information.

Sales person: *'I might be able to help you with that, but before I look at that more closely how much do XYZ Limited currently supply you with on a monthly basis?'*
Open situation question

In the above example the sales person has regained control of the interview and is probing to get more information by asking an open question eg 'how much do XYZ Limited currently supply you with on a monthly basis?' It is possible that the sales person might be able to buy out the existing contract if he has the authority to do so, and could come up with strong feature and benefit that might encourage the prospective customer to change suppliers.

One of the most common failings in sales people is that the prospective customer will ask a question, or voice an objection, the sales person will answer it and then sit back and wait for the prospective customer to ask another question or put up another objection. The sales person has lost control of the interview. In this situation it becomes very difficult to close the sale.

> Objections and questions should be welcomed because they show interest. They are buying signals.

If you have carried out your discussion stage correctly and diagnosed the need or problem then when objections and questions arise they shouldn't present quite so many problems. Let's return to the golden rules of objection handling and examine them more closely.

GOLDEN RULES ON HANDLING OBJECTIONS

Be prepared for them

You will find that the same objections come up time and time again so be prepared for them. Some objections will be general, for example, objections over the price, or that the prospective customer hasn't got time to talk to you. Others will be specific to your industry.

This might involve delivery dates, quality or specifications of a product. In a legal, accountancy, advertising or other service industry it might involve the level of fees charged and lack of consistency of staff. Know what the usual objections are in your type of industry or sector.

ACTION POINT

Make a list of the objections that usually come up during your sales interviews with prospective customers. If you are new to the role or the company then ask your colleagues what objections they generally meet.

Listen to the objection

When a prospective customer voices an objection, listen carefully and patiently in order to understand what the objection is and to avoid argument. Don't even begin to think how you are going to answer yet. Simply listen.

TOP TIPS

Show that you are listening by giving good eye contact with the prospective customer. Lean slightly towards him and angle your head.

On the telephone you can make the listening noises eg 'uh huh', 'I see', but not too many. Concentrate on what the prospective customer is saying.

Don't take the objection personally

Get your inner voice right by saying to yourself something along the lines of, 'I can handle this', 'I can deal with this objection.' Don't become defensive. Tell yourself how far down the positive buying motivations you are and that objections show interest. The prospective customer has the right to make objections.

Ask open questions to probe the objection

Your instinct on hearing the objection might be to leap in and defend your company, or to present a feature and benefit that you think could satisfy the prospective customer and counter his objection. Resist it.

TOP TIPS

Ask the prospective customer an open question to probe the objection. You need to test if it is a sincere objection or a fob off.

In addition, people don't always express themselves well. Are you sure you know exactly what the real objection is?

Alternatively, you might be mentally struggling on how to answer the objection. Asking an open question can not only buy you time while you think of how to answer it but it will also give you more information. Your prospective customer will also need to explain more precisely what he means.

The open question can simply be along the lines of:

'What do you mean by that?'

'What makes you say that?'

'Really, why is that?'

EXAMPLE

Prospective customer: *'You're too expensive.'*
Objection
Sales person: *'What do you mean by too expensive?'*
Open question

The prospective customer will need to explain what he means by 'too expensive' and elaborate on this providing the sales person with more information, for example 'I can get it much cheaper from ABC.'

Now we learn that the prospective customer is comparing your prices with a competitor. Find out what he is really saying. Is it that he hasn't got any money or that he can get it cheaper elsewhere, as in this example? Or has the prospective customer misunderstood you, or does he have a preconception of your pricing that is totally inaccurate?

Ensure that you are listening to the prospective customer and that your mind isn't racing on ahead to give a benefit that is inappropriate.

TOP TIPS

Never assume you know what they mean. If you ASSUME you make an ASS of U and an ASS of ME! Always probe the objection.

By probing and asking questions you can get back into the discussion phase of the sales interview and glean more information until you finally uncover what the true objection is. Only when you know what this is and fully understand what is being said can you proceed to the next stage.

In my experience sales people are often too ready to jump in with their benefits before finding out what the real objection is.

Give your compensating benefit

Once you have all the information you need from the prospective customer, and you have fully understood the objection, then you can draw on your features and benefits and give the compensating benefit to counteract the objection. And if there is no compensating benefit, then simply say so.

You might also be able to use the technique of agreeing with the prospective customer, ie with his thoughts rather than the objection. For example: 'I can understand what are you saying Mr Jones, and some of our best customers used to think the same, but they've found that the benefits of the product far outweighs the higher price in terms of superiority of performance. And you mentioned earlier how important that element was to your business.'

Be sincere and honest

Do not 'flannel.' If there is a genuine disadvantage admit it. Then stress the advantages to the prospective customer to outweigh the disadvantage. Here you may have to draw on information you gained in the sales interview discussion stage.

EXAMPLE

Prospective customer: *'You're too expensive.'*
Sales person: *'What do mean by too expensive?'*
Prospective customer: *'I can get it much cheaper from ABC.'*
Sales person: *'Yes, you're right we are more expensive than ABC, your current suppliers. However, you mentioned earlier that service was very important to you. By paying that extra you are guaranteed a 24 hour service, which means you will be saving money by having less downtime, and you will not be losing customers as a result. We can also arrange payment terms for you so that we can spread the costs over a longer period. If we could delay the first payment for you, so that you don't have to pay until the beginning of your new financial year, would this help you?'*

Now let's take a more detailed look at this.

Admit the disadvantage: 'Yes, you're right we are more expensive than your current suppliers.'

Draw on information gained at the discussion and diagnosis stage: 'However you mentioned earlier that service was very important to you.'

Give compensating feature and benefit: 'By paying that extra you are guaranteed a 24 hour service, which means you will be saving money by having less downtime and you will not be losing customers as a result.'

Strengthen by giving additional advantage or benefit: 'We can also arrange payment terms for you so that we can spread the costs over a longer period.'

And now for the final part:

Converting the objection and closing: 'And if we could delay the first payment for you so that you don't have to pay until the beginning of your new financial year would this help you?'

Convert the objection into a question and make it the basis of the close.

Here, we have asked the prospective customer if he would be interested in the proposition *if* a way can be found of solving his problem. If the objection is insincere then the prospective customer will probably raise another objection. Ignore the first objection and repeat the process on the basis of the second objection.

If the prospective customer keeps raising objections then you probably haven't carried out the following stages of the sales interview adequately enough:

Approach
Discussion
Diagnosis

If this happens ask an open situation question, or ask yourself whether this person is really the decision maker.

HANDLING COMMON OBJECTIONS

As I mentioned before the same objections come up again and again. You will have some that are specific to your industry, service or product, others that are general. So let's take a look at some common examples of objections and how to handle them.

Objection: 'Sorry, no budget.'

Probe. Make it specific. Ask, 'When will you be putting your budgets together?' If you know when their budget process begins perhaps you can demonstrate how you can help them to save money or plan ahead.

Objection: 'How can your company handle a contract like this? You're much too small.'
Probe. Make it specific. Ask, 'What do you mean by too small?' What are they really saying? Are they worried that your company won't be able to fulfil their requirements? Or could there be another reason. Once you have found out the real objection you can handle it by giving your compensating benefits. In this case you could mention names of other customers you deal with which the prospective customer might be able to identify with and therefore reassure him that you really can handle his needs.

Once you have found out what the real objection is then answer it with the compensating benefit.

TELEPHONE SALES CALL OBJECTIONS

There are some objections you will meet on the telephone sales call. The golden rules of objection handling still apply: listen, be positive, don't argue or disagree, and acknowledge them. Depending on the type of objection you can also probe by asking an open question as shown in the previous examples above. There are, however, some objections you will need to accept. Here are a few examples:

Objection: 'We're perfectly happy with our current suppliers.'
If they are then there is little you can do about it, but at least they now know about you. Respect their view and ask if you could send some literature for them to retain on their files. And ask whether you can keep in touch, say every six months. Their needs might change, they might fall out with their current suppliers or they might have a need the current supplier can't satisfy. You want to make sure that if this happens your company is the one on the tip of their tongue to use instead.

Objection: 'We used your company before. It was a total disaster!'
Before you leap in and say 'Well of course we've changed our procedures since then' to which they might answer, 'Since last week?' You need to ask *when* they used you and *what* happened. (Open questions)

Apologise on behalf of your organisation and then concentrate on doing a good public relations exercise. Tell them what has been changed since they used you and how you'd like to win their business again. You may not win them over on this call but you will certainly help to build bridges for a future successful relationship.

Objection: 'Our buying is done through our head office.'
Get the name of the person you should speak to in head office and the telephone number. You can then use the name of the contact you have just spoken to as an introduction to the person in head office. That should help you to get through.

Objection: 'Just send me a brochure.'
This is an objection that is often used on the telephone sales call to avoid agreeing to an appointment. Is this a fob off or is it genuine? Try and push it by saying something like, 'I'd love to put a brochure in the post but we have a wide range of products and many brochures, and if you're like me you haven't got time to wade through them all. So, why don't I arrange for someone to come and see you, spend half an hour with you and then we can leave you with the most appropriate literature and answer any questions you may have.'

Then you can go on to close the call with the objective of getting the appointment by adding, 'So when would be convenient – this week or next week?'

When handling objections remember to probe. Ask 'Why?' Use good open questions to get all the facts.

ACTION POINT

Return to the list of objections you compiled earlier.

Now list what sort of open questions you could ask to probe further.

Looking at the features and benefits of what you offer, how do you think you might answer these objections?

If you meet a new objection and you feel you didn't handle it well then after the sales visit or telephone sales call write it down and then think about how you should have answered it. Ask your colleagues what they would have said and the next time it comes up you will be better prepared to answer it.

Learn from your mistakes. And remember you can't win them all!

QUICK RECAP

- *Objections can come at any time but if you get the* discussion *and* diagnosis *stage of the sales structure correct you are likely to eliminate some of these.*
- *The same objections come up time after time. Be prepared for them.*
- *Don't take objections personally; don't argue or disagree with them.*
- *Get a good inner dialogue going and welcome objections, they show interest.*
- *Make objections specific; ask probing, open questions.*
- *Admit a disadvantage, if there is one, and go on to give a compensating benefit.*
- *Strengthen with another feature and benefit that will appeal to the prospective customer.*
- *If you make a mistake learn from it and do better next time.*

CHAPTER 12

Closing the sale

Closing the sale is often considered to be the most difficult part of the sales interview, and without successfully closing you won't get the business. The close should follow logically from the sales presentation without any hesitation. However, I know that for many people closing is not easy. This chapter will provide you with some simple techniques to help you successfully close the sale.

THE RIGHT ATTITUDE

Years ago, as a rookie sales woman, I had a dread of closing. I told myself I couldn't do it, that I would never get the business. I was fine on everything else, building rapport, asking questions, diagnosing the need, but asking for the order was a nightmare. Then I told myself that 'closing' as a word was out and all I was doing was helping the prospective customer to buy. I told myself that I had an excellent product and I could genuinely help a company by selling this product to them. This changed my outlook and made it far easier for me to sell to the prospective customer.

Having the right inner dialogue and attitude is vital for closing the sale.

CLOSING TECHNIQUES

Simply asking for the business can be the easiest way of closing the sale. For example:

'Can I go ahead and place the order then?'
or
'Shall I start working on this project right away?'
or
'How soon would you like me to start?'

Often the fear of rejection prevents us from asking for the business outright. However, if your sales interview has gone well in that you've built a good rapport with the prospective customer, asked the right questions, diagnosed his needs and sold in the correct features and benefits, the close should follow on naturally.

TOP TIPS

One simple way of closing is to ask for the business. Often the fear of rejection prevents us. Be positive and have a confident manner.

There are some other techniques that can help you to 'ask' for the business and thereby close the sale, which we will cover in this chapter.

Solving the problem close

I looked briefly at this closing technique earlier – if you could solve the prospective customer's problem or objection would he buy?

EXAMPLE

A brewery sales staff found that the following objections came up with some of their prospective customers:

Prospective customer: *'I'm a bit wary about using a small independent brewery like yours?'*
Objection

Sales person: *'Why is that?'*
Probe with an open question

Prospective customer: *'Will you be able to deliver the quantities I require?'*

Sales person: *'Yes, we can, and do regularly to other public houses of a similar size to yours and larger.'*
Provide testimonials and relevant features and benefits

Prospective customer: *'But you only deliver on a Thursday and Thursday is my day off.'*
Another objection

Sales person: *'So if we could arrange delivery for you at the beginning of the week would you be prepared to order through us?'*

Solving the prospect's problem close

Prospective customer: *'I suppose if you could deliver on Tuesday that would be OK.'*

Sales person (with pen in hand and order forms to the ready): *'Right, Tuesday it is. How many barrels would you like to order for the first delivery? Six or 12?'*

(This is another closing technique – the alternative close. See below for more details on this technique)

Prospective customer: *'Better make it 15.'*

Sale completed.

In this example the sales person used two closing techniques. Initially he used the *solving the prospect's problem close* but then he added another close, he asked the prospect how many barrels he would like giving him an *alternative* to choose from.

The alternative close

Giving the prospective customer an alternative to choose from will make it easier for him to make a decision.

Here are some further examples of this alternative close.

- 'So when would you like delivery, this week or next week?'
- 'Which colour would you prefer, green or blue?'
- 'How would you like to pay? By cheque or credit card?'

This is a very useful technique and one that also works well in closing in the telephone sales call. For example:

- 'When would be the best time to call and see you, this week or next week?'
- 'What would suit you better? Morning or afternoon?'

EXAMPLE

The telephone sales person in our contact lens manufacturer example could close by saying:

'Why don't I set up a trial run for you so that you can test us out before making a firm commitment? When would you like to start? Today or tomorrow?'
Or
'If I can take your order now I can have those contact lenses with you tomorrow. How many packs would you like to order, six or 12?'
Or
'Why don't I come and see you then we can run through the order list, set up the paperwork and I can answer any more questions you have, as well as show you samples. When would be convenient, Wednesday or Friday?'

TOP TIPS

Give the prospective customer an alternative to choose from when closing, especially when seeking to make an appointment, eg days, weeks, times, morning or afternoon. It helps them to make a decision.

The free trial close

Maybe you can offer something free for them to try, as in our contact lens manufacturer example, where the objective of the telephone sales call is to get the optician to accept a free trial. If the optician agrees then the lenses are dispatched and another follow up call made to see how satisfied the customer is with them with the aim of trying to win a firm order.

Some shipping and printing companies offer a free quotation as a close. They ask the prospective customer to either fax or email them their last order and provide a quote for comparison purposes, with the objective of bettering that price and so winning the business.

ACTION POINT

Think about your products or services: can you offer the prospective customer the chance to attend a free demonstration, or can you provide a free quote, or send free samples?

The fear close

Then there is the fear close, used to put pressure on the prospective customer to make an immediate decision or risk losing the opportunity of a purchase or a special offer.

For example:
'If you place your order now you will get a 20% discount.'
or
'This special offer only lasts until the end of the week so if you want to take advantage of it you should place your order now.'
or
'We've had a lot of interest in this model. If you leave your decision too long we may have sold out.' (Estate agents and car sales people seem to like this one!)
or
'If you confirm the order now I could put it through with this month's orders which would guarantee you'd get delivery next week.' (I have had this close used on me a few times and it does work. When the sales man threw in a month's free trial he had a deal.)

Other examples along this same thread are:
'I really need this order to boost my sales figures, especially as we close the sales order book for the month today.'
or
'I've got a wife and five children to feed, if I don't get this order I'll be out of a job!'
I'll leave you to decide if you want to use these!

The assumptive close

This is similar to the *solving the problem close.* What you are saying here is that if you can satisfy the prospective customer on a point he has raised would he buy?

EXAMPLE

Sales person: *'Assuming then that we can get this model for you by Tuesday are you prepared to go ahead and place the order, Mr Jones?'*

Prospective customer: *'Yes.'*

Sales person: *'Right, I will just make a call to our depot and see if I can arrange that for you.'*

Another example:
Sales person: *'Assuming then that you are satisfied that complete confidentiality is guaranteed will you buy from us?'*

If the prospective customer says that he is not sure then there are some other underlying objections that you have not uncovered. You need to find out what these are and resolve them. Ask an open question and probe the objection, for example: 'What aren't you sure about, Mr Jones?' Then handle the objection as detailed in the previous chapter and try closing again.

The buying signals close

As I have previously mentioned, buying signals can come through at any time during the sales interview by a show of interest. This can be in the form of the prospective customer asking you questions, or even by raising objections. But it may also be in the form of expressions such as, 'oh' or 'really.' Alternatively you might see it in the prospective customer's body language. And on the telephone you might pick it up by the intonation in the voice, which conveys interest.

By capitalising on these buying signals you can go on to close. However, many sales people are concentrating so hard on making their points that they can miss these vital buying signals. Look for them and listen for them. When you hear them, repeat or strengthen the benefit to the prospect and then close with one of the techniques mentioned above.

TOP TIPS

Regardless of which technique is suitable for you, remember that closing the sale begins with the approach stage. If you don't create the right first impression and establish and build rapport you will not be able to close the sale and come away with the business.

When you have closed the sale the tendency is to talk on and then oversell. **Don't.** Tell the customer what you are going to do next: eg put an order form on the fax/email/in the post, ring them back in six months' time, send a representative to see them etc.

Make sure you have all the relevant details. Then c**hange the subject, and get out (or finish the call).**

Different customers, different situations and different products and services call for different techniques, only you can judge at the time which is the correct one to use. Whichever one seems appropriate, be sincere, honest and genuine and you will not only win the business but gain repeat business and recommendations.

QUICK RECAP

- *Be positive and have a confident manner. Don't be afraid to ask for the business.*
- *One closing technique involves solving the prospective customer's problem to help him to buy.*
- *The* ***alternative close*** *makes it easier for people to make a decision.*
- *The* ***fear close*** *puts pressure on the prospective customer to make a decision or lose out in some way.*
- *Look and listen for buying signals and capitalise on them by strengthening your benefit and going on to ask for the business.*
- *Beware of the tendency to talk on and oversell.*
- *Having won the business, change the subject and depart gracefully.*
- *Being sincere, honest and genuine will not only win you the business but gain repeat business and recommendations.*

CHAPTER 13

Selling to different personalities

Finally, I return to the maxim 'People buy people.' I say 'finally' but this is by no means the least important aspect in the selling process. It is in fact extremely important. If someone likes you they are more inclined to buy from you. But everyone is different. So how do you get people to like you? How do you successfully sell to those people who are not like you?

This chapter examines the different personality types and shows you how to recognise them, and how to respond to them in order to win the business. It also looks at the different styles of communication between men and women in a sales situation.

UNDERSTANDING PERSONALITIES

Everyone is different. You think you are 'normal' but what is 'normal'? Normal is different to each and every one of us. We see the world through our own eyes, we think everyone should behave, act and be like us. Well, of course that isn't so. We all have different personalities. Understanding and recognising this can help you adapt your approach to another person and get on their wavelength. This in turn can greatly aid the selling process.

> To be a good sales person you need to have an understanding of people and the knowledge that different things will motivate different people.

In order to provide you with a greater understanding I am going to look at a fairly simple model which was devised by William Marston in 1926, and which is still used today. Whilst people are highly complex and certainly more complex than the descriptions I am going to give you, this model will, I hope, help you see yourself and others in a different light, and so, enable you to change tactics to communicate more effectively, build a better rapport with your prospective customers and win the sale.

PERSONALITY TYPES

There are four basic personality types:

- Type A: Dominant
- Type B: Social
- Type C: Measured
- Type D: Compliant

Personality traits are inherited; however this can be influenced by other factors such as upbringing, environment, and education. You should also take into consideration a person's intellectual capacity and their behaviour; both of these will affect how they react and relate to you and likewise you to them.

Although we may contain a mixture of the personality traits I below examine some will be stronger than others. This will, to some extent, dictate how we communicate and behave.

ACTION POINT

See if you can recognise yourself from the descriptions on the following pages. Then think about how you might need to change your approach towards a prospective customer in order to build better rapport with him and therefore come away with the business.

TYPE A: DOMINANT PERSONALITIES

Type A personalities have dominance and superiority in their make up. This makes them rather impatient individuals. They are very direct people who 'speak as they find' and 'don't suffer fools gladly.' They are confident decision makers (although these may not always be the right decisions) but there is no pussy-footing around with these types. They are extremely time conscious and find it hard to relax. They are always doing something and even on holiday, if they take one, will want to be using the time 'wisely.' They can be rather intolerant of others who are slower than them.

Their body language will often be very positive and can sometimes be overpowering, as can their manner of speaking. You might find them rather abrupt, and if speaking to them on the telephone could think them rude, but this might not necessarily be so. It is just their manner.

The superiority in their personality makes them less able to understand and relate to others who aren't like them. Dominants can also be ambitious people so you could find them at the top of the hierarchy. They are not really team players, even if they say they are, their team is often just one member – themselves. They like being in control and will often take charge in a group situation. They usually have lots of ideas, thrive on change, and like solving problems. They do not like a lot of detail but prefer to leave this to others.

Recognising dominant individuals

You may already have a good idea of how to recognise a dominant individual by the description above. But here are some further tips to help you:

- Their handshake will often be outstretched taking up more space than is normal and their grip will be very firm.
- They could position their hand so that it is on top of yours.
- They could give you the double clutch handshake – the 'politician's handshake'.
- They could touch the top of your arm when shaking hands.
- They may hold on to your hand longer than is usual.
- They may be sitting well back in their chair with their hands clasped behind their head.
- They will give you very direct eye contact.

They will not make time for social chit-chat but will want to get straight to the point. They will make flat assertions like 'You're too expensive', or 'Come on sell to me', and will enjoy putting you on the spot. They are quick decision makers and will want to close the sale there and then.

EXAMPLE

I was visiting a prospective marketing client. He was a large man and I could see immediately he had a great deal of presence. He shook hands with me giving me very direct eye contact. His grip was extremely firm and his arm outstretched. I returned the pressure and found him saying, 'My goodness you've got a firm handshake.' My response was to say, 'I can give as good as I get.' He smiled and said, 'You've got the business.' I didn't need to do anything more to win this client. He liked my direct response and perceived I was like him and would get the job done.

Selling to dominant individuals

Dominant personalities are motivated by status so it is likely they will have the status symbols such as the big car, the big office and chair, or the expensive watch and designer accessories.

They can also have an ego. Here the prospective customer is not just saying, 'I am important,' but 'I am *even more* important', so if you miss out those situation questions, asking them about themselves, and/or their business then you've blown it. Make sure however that your questions are businesslike, relevant and to the point.

In addition, you will need to fully satisfy the subjective reasons for buying, which we examined earlier, ie the need to satisfy and feed an ego.

When selling to dominant personalities don't give them the detail. For example, don't go through the proposal step-by-step or they will quickly get bored and irritated and cut you short. Tell them what you're going to do for them and how you're going to save them time, or make them more successful, powerful, or happy, etc.

TOP TIPS

Adopt a businesslike manner; be crisp and efficient, but obviously not unfriendly.

Be clear and specific.

Speed up the way you talk, be direct, and get straight to the point.

Ensure that your handshake is firm and your body language is positive.

Use time efficiently and stick to the business in hand.

Show that you are well prepared and that you know your product/service thoroughly.

TYPE B: SOCIAL PERSONALITIES

The Type B social personality is a 'people-person' and likes to be liked. They find it much easier than any of the other personality types to mirror and match another person's body language because they are more attuned to people's needs and moods. This means they are usually very good sales people. They are adaptable, flexible and participative. They have high energy levels and are articulate, confident and co-operative. They are enthusiastic, embrace ideas, and thrive on change. Their body language will be open and positive.

They are usually highly persuasive individuals but find it hard to deal with confrontation and often struggle to close the business. They will be friendly, talkative and smile at you. Indeed you may have trouble shutting them up! They won't be as direct and forthright as the Type A dominant personality.

They are team players but the adaptability in their personality means they can change their minds.

Recognising social individuals

Status is as important to social personalities as it is to dominant ones so you could still see the big car and the designer accessories. Where you will note a difference though between the two types of personalities is that the social person will go out of his way to make you like him. Look out for the following signs:

- The handshake will be firm but not overpowering, the elbow tucked into the waist.
- They will want to spend time on the pleasantries.
- They will offer you a drink or ensure that you are comfortable.
- They will put you at ease.
- They will smile at you and give friendly eye contact.
- Their body language will be positive, confident and relaxed, not threatening.

Social personality types will often have pictures of their families, achievements and possessions on their walls, much the same as dominants, but when you ask a social personality about a picture he will start chatting to you about it whereas the dominant individual will be unlikely to. The dominant personality will cut the social chit-chat and focus on what you're there for, to do business.

Selling to social individuals

Social personalities are motivated by variety, working with people, ideals and visions, so you will need to show them how your products or services can support those visions and ideals and serve to make them more popular with their colleagues, peers or customers. With regard to the subjective reasons for buying, here you are satisfying the need for respect and approval.

TOP TIPS

Leave plenty of time for socialising at the beginning of the interview.

The **Approach** stage could take much longer because you could end up talking about their family or their golf swing before getting down to the business.

They are not great lovers of detail so put anything technical, or all the details, in writing afterwards.

Provide ideas for helping them.

Pursue a supporting relationship and leave on a friendly social note.

Use positive open body language including maintaining good eye contact.

TYPE C: MEASURED PERSONALITIES

The Type C measured personality is far more logical and analytical than either our A (dominant) or our B (social) personality. They are steady, often security minded and don't like a lot of change. They can be suspicious and sceptical of new ideas and it will take some time to persuade them.

They are consistent, caring and patient. They don't like taking risks and will only do so if they have weighed up all the pros and cons. They are great list makers!

Many engineers fall into this category because they are attracted to that occupation by its analytical, methodical approach. You can also find lawyers, accountants, and professional buyers are this personality type.

Recognising a measured individual

Measured personality types are not motivated by status so the designer accessories and big cars etc will be missing. Their influencing style is logic and reason coupled with facts. You can recognise them by the following:

- Measured individuals can often be slower speaking and more quietly spoken.
- There will be silences in the conversation, which if you have a lot of dominance in your personality can be difficult for you.
- There will be no dominant body language.
- The handshake can be firm or weak.
- Measured individuals will be looking at you rather sceptically.
- They will sit well back in their chair with their arms folded, not necessarily with hostility, but they will be holding back a judgment on you and what you are saying until they have weighed you up, and they are ready to pronounce in their own mind whether they like you or not.
- They will also procrastinate which makes it a lot harder for you to close the sale.

Responding to measured individuals

This is the type of customer who will require all the details from you. You will need to patiently explain the product or service benefits and go through applications and procedures carefully and painstakingly. If you are a dominant personality yourself you will find this very frustrating, but if you don't slow down and provide the prospective customer with this he won't buy from you.

Because of their cautious nature Type C personalities can have a tendency to over-plan. They are generally warm-hearted but when aggressive can be very stubborn and intransigent. They can dig their heels in. Fairness is also paramount.

They will also know a great deal about your product or service having spent weeks or even months researching it before deciding to talk to you. You can't fob them off. When closing you will have to direct them. You will need to help them make up their mind but don't rush them. If you do you will lose the sale completely.

TOP TIPS

Take time to break the ice, find common ground and make yourself agreeable.

Use open questions to get information and draw them out. These are the people who will simply give you a one-word answer if you ask a closed question.

Be sincere and show an interest in the prospective customer as a person.

Take time to find areas of common ground.

Be honest and open, and patiently draw out his goals in a non-threatening manner.

Slow down, and move casually and informally.

Provide lots of assurances and give clear and specific solutions with maximum guarantees.

Give them the detail. If you don't they will ask for it.

Listen without interrupting.

Don't patronise or show irritation.

TYPE D: COMPLIANT PERSONALITIES

The Type D compliant personality likes to comply with the rules and regulations. This means they are usually very systematic, precise, hyper-efficient and bureaucratic. These people love facts and detail, the more the better, and even more than our Type C measured personality.

Their compliant nature means they can often easily agree which makes it difficult for you to know exactly what they are really feeling and thinking. They need to feel completely sure of their position and of others' expectations.

They can give the impression of coldness and disinterest and will use rules, authority and logical argument to influence the actions of others. They have a tendency to correct errors and inaccuracies that others might consider insignificant so you might find them irritating if your personality errs towards the A (dominant) or B (social) type. If you let this show then you will lose the sale.

They are concerned with quality, and do not want to accept inferior work regardless of timescales so make sure you don't overpromise and under deliver.

Recognising a compliant individual

They are punctual and like punctuality in others so if you turn up a few minutes late you could find you've lost the business before you've even had a chance to win it. You can also recognise them by the following:

- They can often be shy and self-effacing with closed and hunched body language.
- You will often get lowered eye contact and fidgeting mannerisms.
- There will be no dominant body language.
- The handshake can be perfunctory and not terribly firm.
- They will speak quietly and can be vague.

Responding to compliant individuals

Compliant individuals need a great deal of detail. They will want a full explanation giving reasons. You will need to give them plenty of time to make up their mind but gently direct them towards the close.

TOP TIPS

Be straightforward in your approach, stick to the business in hand, don't digress into social chit-chat – they don't want it.

Build credibility by listing the pros and cons of any suggestions you make.

Reassure them that there won't be any surprises.

Be realistic and accurate.

Provide solid, tangible, practical evidence in the form of testimonials.

Give them time to make any decisions.

There are, of course, many more complexities of personalities than I have given you here, but I hope this goes some way in helping you to understand that we are all different and because of this we need to accept that different approaches work with different people.

> Being aware of the different personalities, reading the body language, and adapting your approach can help you to win the business.

DIFFERENT STYLES IN COMMUNICATION

Men and women have different styles of communication. You will need to recognise this and play to it in your sales interview.

A woman's style of communication is generally more social than that of a man. By this I mean that women need more background information about one another than men do. When two women meet, particularly for the first time, they will try to establish common ground by talking about their families, their homes, their holidays, their jobs, their bosses, their colleagues and their feelings and thoughts. Men sometimes call this gossiping but it isn't, not to a woman anyway. It is the female style of communication. Some men naturally have this style of communication too and consequently are very good at talking to and selling to women.

Generally though, the male style of communication is far more direct. Men don't need this social background information. They don't need to know about family and home circumstances. They see it as unnecessary.

The more **social personality (Type B)** mentioned in the previous section will, if it is a man, want the social chit-chat but this when man-to-man, will usually be based around four major areas; cars, football or sport, women and work.

If a female has more of the **dominant personality (Type A)** then she will exhibit more of the male style of communication and therefore be more direct in her communication. Quite often women who work in male dominated organisations, and who have reached management positions, have adopted this male style of communication either accidentally or by design.

The sales man

The salesman will need to ascertain whether or not the female prospective customer is a dominant personality. If she is then he will need to respond accordingly by being direct and leaving out the social chit-chat. If she isn't a dominant personality then he would do well to take time to socialise by getting to know the woman as a person, finding out more about her background circumstances, her likes and dislikes etc. Some men are very wary of doing this, as they are afraid that it sounds as if they are 'chatting up' the woman. Those men with very strong male styles of communication find this particularly difficult. All I can advise is that they should practise the open questions. This will help them sound more natural in the socialising process. And remember, this is even more vital if selling to a measured or compliant female. It will take longer and more open questions to break the ice.

The sales woman

If the sales woman is selling to a male prospective customer then unless he has the female style of communication (which she won't know until he starts asking her about her family background, interests or job) she needs to avoid any attempt at the social chit-chat and talk business.

Women need to be more direct in their communication with men. They need to stick to the business in hand. It will be pointless trying to relate to the man by talking about cars or football because even if the woman is the world's expert on both these subjects it is unlikely the man will respond. Football and cars are part of the male communication process and a woman talking on these matters can often be viewed as invading that territory and therefore could be considered something of a threat.

TOP TIPS

Be attuned to the prospective customer's personality and communication styles and adapt your own to build and establish rapport. The sales interview is not about you or what you want but about the prospective customer and how you can help him.

QUICK RECAP

- *People buy people so enhancing the likeability factor can help you to win the sale.*
- *We are all different. Understanding and recognising the different personalities and then adapting your approach can make you more successful in selling.*
- *To be a good sales person you need to have an understanding of people.*
- *You should take into consideration a person's personality, their intellectual capacity and their behaviour, all of which will affect how they react and relate to you and likewise you to them.*
- *There are four basic 'personality types':*
  Type A: Dominant
  Type B: Social
  Type C: Measured
  Type D: Compliant
- *Recognising the different personalities and responding correctly to them can help drive the sales process forward.*
- *A woman's communication style means she will generally need more background information about the person she is doing business with than a man normally requires.*
- *The male style of communication is far more direct. Men don't need the background information.*
- *Men selling to women should take more time to find out about the woman as a person, whilst women selling to men should be more direct in their approach.*

PART 3

FURTHER RESOURCES

CHAPTER 14

Quickstart guide: summary of key points

PART ONE: PLANNING FOR THE SALE

CHAPTER 1: UNDERSTANDING SELLING

- Selling is a means of persuading or influencing your customers and prospective customers to purchase your company's services or products rather than someone else's.
- Marketing means identifying, anticipating, communicating and satisfying your customers' requirements profitably.
- Sales representatives and business owners often need to generate and qualify leads, cold-call to make sales appointments, and sell face-to-face to the prospective customer.
- Leads can come from a variety of sources.
- Selling is a skill; it can be learnt, practised and honed.
- People need to see the benefits of what you are offering before they decide whether or not to make a purchase.
- With the right training, and an awareness and understanding of others, most people can become good sales people.
- A good sales person needs:
  - Professionalism
  - An excellent knowledge of his products or services
  - An awareness of his competitors and the marketplace
  - An awareness of his customers' needs and wants
  - Superb skills in managing communications. eg being a good listener and having the ability to ask the correct questions
  - The ability to build rapport quickly and effectively
  - Persistence
- When selling face-to-face you will need to project a confident image through your appearance and body language.
- When selling over the telephone you will need to project a confident image through your voice.

CHAPTER 2: BUYER BEHAVIOUR AND MOTIVATION

- Understanding how buyers behave will give you greater knowledge in the sales process and therefore make you better equipped to convert the sale.
- Individuals will buy products or services to satisfy the basic physiological needs. These are the objective reasons why people buy.
- Individuals will also be looking to satisfy the psychological needs. These are the subjective reasons.
- In order to sell a service you need to be both personally acceptable and have expertise.
- Selling a service, particularly a professional service, is highly personal.
- There are two sets of buying motivations: Positive and Negative.
- In order to win business you will need to switch the prospective customer over to the positive buying motivations.

CHAPTER 3: PRODUCT AND MARKET KNOWLEDGE

- In order to be an effective sales person you need to have good product knowledge.
- You need to know the features of what you are offering and the benefits of those features.
- You need to examine this on two levels: firstly your organisational level and secondly at an individual product/service level.
- Prospective customers will want to know what makes your company different. Why should they buy from you?
- What you are selling is one or more of the following:
  - The solution to a problem.
  - Something that will fulfil a need.
  - Something that will make someone happier or feel good.

  - Something that will make a business more efficient or life easier and more enjoyable.
- The two magic words which turn a feature into a benefit are 'which means'.
- Continually research and monitor your marketplace and your competitors.

CHAPTER 4: REACHING THE DECISION MAKER

- You may have to go through several people in one company before reaching the decision maker, this is called the Decision Making Unit (DMU).
- The DMU may contain some, or even, all of the following: Gatekeepers, Users, Influencers, Buyers, Deciders, and Specifiers.
- The Gatekeepers are the people who think they are paid to keep you out.
- You will more frequently come up against the Gatekeeper if you are cold-calling either personally or on the telephone.
- Your first objective is to get through to the decision maker, be clear about this from the start as it will come through in your voice.
- Believe in what you are selling, don't hesitate, keep your talking to a minimum, put pressure on the telephonist to put you through; the name of the person you wish to speak to and your name is all the information he requires. Don't respond to their questions but ask questions yourself.
- Every person you speak to away from the decision maker weakens the sale and what you have said will be misinterpreted.
- Finding the right person to sell to, or going through the various people in the DMU, requires a methodical and persistent approach.

- Ask if the person you are seeing is the decision maker. This will help you to establish if you need to involve anyone else in the sales presentation, or if you need to return to make another sales presentation.

CHAPTER 5: PREPARING FOR THE SALES CALL AND VISIT

- Plan who you are targeting.
- Putting your target audience into easily identifiable groups will help you target, measure and analyse the results of your calls.
- Different groups of customers will be available at varying times throughout the day so make sure you stagger your calls.
- The more you know about the industries you are targeting and their practices the more informed you will be about the best times to call them.
- Be realistic about how many sales calls or sales visits you can make in one day.
- It is far better to make good qualified appointments than those just to make numbers up to reach targets.
- Before picking up the telephone to make your call, or going out to the sales interview, set your objective, to be clear what you want to achieve from the sales interview.
- Remember: the higher the value of the purchase the longer it will take to get the sale.
- Research your prospective customer before calling on them.
- Before calling or visiting a prospective customer make sure you have all the necessary leaflets, price lists and brochures to hand. Prepare as well as you can before any sales interview.

PART TWO: THE SALES STRUCTURE

CHAPTER 6: THE SALES STRUCTURE – APPROACH

- On the telephone sales call make your introduction as succinct as possible. You should say your name and your company name clearly and slowly and also say briefly what your company does.
- Smile while you dial! A smile lifts your voice and gives it more enthusiasm.
- Build rapport with your caller by matching the speed of their voice, vary your pitch and make sure you do not sound droll.
- Look and be alert. If your body is slouched your voice will sound slouched.
- Use the same body language on the telephone as you would normally face-to-face.
- On the face-to-face sales interview arrive early for an appointment and see what you can glean about that organisation in reception.
- If the prospective customer is visiting you at your premises, or coming to your exhibition stand, make sure it is giving out the correct impression.
- You begin to close the sale the first few seconds you meet the prospective customer so first impressions are critical.
- Ensure your appearance is appropriate and you are well groomed. The golden rule to ask yourself is: Where am I going? Who am I seeing? What do I wear?
- 55% of the impression you make on other people is based on your appearance and your body language so take time to get this right.
- When greeting the prospective customer walk forwards with your arm outstretched, not too stiff but with your elbow tucked into your waist, smile and give good eye contact. Your handshake should be firm and dry.

- Sit only when invited. Keep your body language open and sit back in the chair. Do not put anything on the prospective customer's desk or table without asking. The desk or table is their territory and you are invading it if you don't have permission.
- Set the tone for the sales interview by starting with neutral remarks.

CHAPTER 7: THE SALES STRUCTURE – DISCUSSION

- In order to switch the prospective customer from the negative buying motivations: '*I don't trust you*', '*I don't need you*' to the positive ones: '*I am important*', '*Consider my needs*' you need to get them talking by asking open questions.
- Open questions are those that cannot be answered with a simple 'yes' or 'no'. They begin with: 'who', 'what', 'why', 'how', 'when', 'where'.
- Closed questions, which begin with: 'is/are', 'will/would', 'could/can', 'should/shall' and 'did/do' can be used to obtain clarification or to elicit a specific response.
- The discussion phase on the telephone sales interview is shorter than in the face-to-face sales interview.
- On the telephone you need to engage the prospective customer's attention quickly by asking fewer open questions and by starting with an open attention question.
- Open situation questions are designed to probe the situation.
- Keep your questions in front of you when making your telephone calls.
- You cannot sell your product or service until you have information. Miss out this vital first stage and you will miss the sale!
- Keep control of the interview at all times by using good questioning techniques, in particular open questions.

- Don't hand your literature to a prospective customer at the beginning of the sale, save it until the end of the sales process.
- Be careful about asking multiple questions and value-loaded questions.
- Leading questions can be used in some circumstances where you want to lead the prospective customer into giving a positive response and to close the sales interview.

CHAPTER 8: THE SALES STRUCTURE: DIAGNOSIS, IMPLICATIONS AND NEEDS

- Use problem or need questions to identify areas of need and problems.
- Once you have the information you can then introduce the appropriate benefit that will help to solve the prospective customer's problems or satisfy the needs you have uncovered.
- Comparative questions can give you more information and can help you explore different angles.
- Summarising skills enable the prospective customer to see that you have listened and correctly understood the situation.
- Don't oversell. Give only the features and benefits that are relevant and of interest to the prospective customer.
- Questions are a buying signal – welcome them. Answer them honestly and openly.
- Acknowledge the question and then ask an open question if you need more information.

CHAPTER 9: BODY LANGUAGE

- Body language can be used to create an impression, you can read what the other person is thinking and feeling through their body language.
- You need to be aware of your own body language and be able to interpret the use of the prospect's body language.

- You can also use body language to build rapport with the prospect.
- Personal distance varies from country to country, don't invade the prospective customer's personal space.
- If the prospective customer leans forward when you say something it shows interest. This is a buying signal, capitalise on it by strengthening your benefit and asking open questions.
- If the prospective customer sits back, folds his arms or rubs his ears that means he doesn't much like what you are saying, ask an open question to get the prospective customer talking or to find out why they aren't keen on what you are saying.
- Avoid defensive gestures, ie closed body language. This means crossed legs, crossed arms and sitting well back and stiffly in your seat.
- Maintain good eye contact with your prospective customer throughout the sales interview.
- If you need to take notes always ask if you can first. Don't take too many, as you will lose eye contact with the prospect.
- You can also build rapport by subtly mirroring the prospective customer's body language.

CHAPTER 10: LISTENING SKILLS

- Listening is an essential part of being a good sales person.
- The good sales person listens to the prospective customer. There is a saying – you have two ears and one mouth. You should be listening twice as much as you are talking.
- Listening involves:
  - The ability to understand what is being said.
  - The ability to organise and analyse the messages in order to retain them for subsequent use.
- There are two types of listening: casual listening and critical listening.

- There are many reasons why we don't listen properly: physical tiredness or discomfort, desire to talk, different perspectives, strong emotions and prejudices, preconceived ideas, reactions to the speaker and simple distractions and mind wandering.
- It takes practice and concentration to listen properly.
- The good sales person does not judge anyone but keeps an open mind.

CHAPTER 11: HANDLING OBJECTIONS

- Objections can come at any time but if you get the discussion and diagnosis stage of the sales structure correct you are likely to eliminate some of these.
- The same objections come up time after time. Be prepared for them.
- Don't take objections personally; don't argue or disagree with them.
- Get a good inner dialogue going and welcome objections, they show interest.
- Make objections specific; ask probing, open questions.
- Admit a disadvantage if there is one and go on to give a compensating benefit.
- Strengthen with another feature and benefit that will appeal to the prospective customer.
- If you make a mistake learn from it and do better next time.

CHAPTER 12: CLOSING THE SALE

- Be positive and have a confident manner. Don't be afraid to ask for the business.
- One closing technique involves solving the prospective customer's problem to help him to buy.
- The alternative close makes it easier for people to make a decision.

- The fear close puts pressure on the prospect to make a decision or lose out in some way.
- Look and listen for buying signals and capitalise on them by strengthening your benefit and going on to ask for the business.
- Beware of the tendency to talk on and oversell.
- Having won the business, change the subject and depart gracefully.
- Being sincere, honest and genuine will not only win you the business but gain repeat business and recommendations.

CHAPTER 13: SELLING TO DIFFERENT PERSONALITIES

- People buy people so enhancing the likeability factor can help you to win the sale.
- We are all different. Understanding and recognising the different personalities and then adapting your approach can make you more successful in selling.
- To be a good sales person you need to have an understanding of people.
- You should take into consideration a person's personality, their intellectual capacity and their behaviour all of which will affect how they react and relate to you and likewise you to them.
- There are four basic 'personality types':
  Type A: Dominant
  Type B: Social
  Type C: Measured
  Type D: Compliant
- Recognising the different personalities and responding correctly to them can help drive the sales process forward.
- A woman's communication style means she will generally

need more background information about the person she is doing business with than a man requires.

- The male style of communication is far more direct. Men don't need the background information.
- Men selling to women should take more time to find out about the woman as a person, whilst women selling to men should be more direct in their approach.

CHAPTER 15

Troubleshooting

Q: I've been asked to make some telephone sales calls to follow up a mailshot. I am having difficulty in getting the appointment and keep being told by prospective customers that they'll contact me if they need me. How can I overcome this?

A: I always think it is difficult to follow up a mailshot because, if you're not careful, you end up asking a closed question right at the beginning of the sales call instead of asking an open question. Let's look at a few examples of open and closed questions.

For example: If you begin your telephone sales call with your name and introduction and then commence the call with: 'We recently sent you a brochure about our products, did you receive it?', the conversation can go two ways:

Version one

Prospective customer: 'Yes, thanks. We'll keep it on file and call you when we need you.'

There is little you can do except acknowledge this. If you start to press them along the lines of: 'Have you any idea of when that might be?' this is what you might get in response: 'Not at the moment. We'll let you know.'

Let's take a closer look at this example:

Telephone sales person: 'We recently sent you a brochure about our products, **did** you receive it?' This is a closed question. The answer can either be, 'yes' or 'no'. In the above case the prospective customer answered, 'yes,' but went on to tell you that he'll keep it on file and that he'll call you when he needs you.

Telephone sales person: '**Have** you any idea of when that might be?' Again, this is a closed question. In this example the prospective customer answered: 'Not at the moment. We'll let you know.'

Version two

Telephone sales person: 'We recently sent you a brochure about our products, did you receive it?'

Prospective customer: 'No.'
Telephone sales person: 'It provided details of our wide range of stationery products at very competitive prices and with free delivery. If you order over £50 before the end of the month you will also get a free luxury food hamper. Is this something you'd be interested in?'

Now let's examine this example in more detail:
Telephone sales person: 'We recently sent you a brochure about our products, **did** you receive it?' **This is a closed question.**
Prospective customer: 'No.'
Telephone sales person: 'It provided details of our wide range of stationery products at very competitive prices and with free delivery. If you order over £50 before the end of the month you will also get a free luxury food hamper. Is this something you'd be interested in?' The sales person launched into his sales spiel and then followed it up with another closed question.

If you follow up a mailshot then make sure you ask an opening attention question as soon as possible and follow it up with open questions.

Depending on what the mailshot is about it can sometimes be easier to treat the call as a cold-call and that way, if the customer has seen the mailshot, your call will only serve to reinforce what he has already seen, therefore strengthening the sale.

However, let's look at some ways you could follow up a brochure mailshot by starting with an opening attention question to stimulate discussion:

Telephone sales person: 'We recently sent you a brochure providing details of our wide range of stationery items. **How** often do you place a stationery order, Mr Jones?'

(Opening attention question)

Prospective customer: 'About once a month.'

Telephone sales person: '**How** much do you typically spend?'

(Open situation question)

Prospective customer: 'About £40.'

Telephone sales person: 'If you haven't already ordered this month, and can make that order up to £50, we're offering free delivery *and* a free luxury food hamper. **How** does that sound to you?'

(Open question with benefit and the offer of a free gift – another benefit).

Think through your call beforehand to see how you can approach it by using open questions. The more you get the person talking the greater your success in getting the order or the appointment, or at the least getting useful information to qualify the lead or follow it up again at a later date.

Q: I am usually quite successful in selling but there are some prospective customers I find extremely difficult to deal with and my conversion rate therefore is very low. How can I overcome this?

A: Firstly, define which types of customers you find particularly difficult to deal with. Write a list of their characteristics. For example, are they quick-speaking individuals or more slowly speaking and methodical? What is their body language like, overbearing or more submissive? Are there some personality traits that keep reoccurring?

Next, compile a list of your own characteristics. For example, do you like to know all the facts before you make a decision, or are you a quick decision-maker? Do you enjoy variety and change, or would you prefer to know exactly what you are doing and when? If you find this difficult to do, then ask a trusted friend or colleague to compile a list of what they believe to be your characteristics.

Below is a quick checklist to help you. You might like to tick against those personality traits you've already identified from drawing up your lists above and add some additional ones to your lists.

Type A: Dominant	Type B: Social	Type C: Measured	Type D: Compliant
• Dominant • Makes flat assertions, eg 'That's rubbish', 'That will never happen' • Authoritative • Asks direct questions • Superior • Intolerant of time wasters – interrupts and keeps looking at his watch • Lacks patience, easily angered, fidgets • Achiever • Strong autocrat • Not a team player • Solver of problems • Doesn't like detail • Makes quick decisions	• Social – likes people and likes to be liked • Adaptable • Participative • Articulate • Co-operative • Enthusiastic/ embraces ideas • Likes to please • Flexible • A mind changer • Good team player • Likes to be involved in lots of different things with lots of different people	• Steady • Consistent • Security minded • Measured approach/ procrastinates • Sceptical • Patient • Can be silent • Cautious • Suspicious of new ideas • Efficient • Non-risk taker • Reliable • A plodder • Likes stability • Needs time to adapt to change	• Compliant • Systematic • Hyper-efficient • Bureaucratic • Precise • Detailed • Punctual • Shy/self-effacing • Needs assurance • Easily agreeing • Acquiescent • Can have difficulty expressing himself, talks in a vague/meandering style • Superficially helpful and understanding • Likes harmony • Needs a detailed brief and explanation of reasons • Lots of time to think about things

Now consider the prospective customers you find particularly difficult to deal with, are they different to your own personality?

If the prospective customers you find difficult to deal with are quick-speaking, dominant people (Type A) and you are a steadier and slower speaking individual, and like providing the detail (Type C) then it is not surprising that you find this type of prospective customer difficult to deal with, you are opposite personalities. In order to win the business here you will need to practise speeding up the way you talk, which I know can be difficult, but it can be achieved. One way to do this is to practise being more direct with your answers, and with presenting your features and benefits. Know the features and benefits thoroughly before meeting the prospective customer and rehearse them. Practise keeping your body language open and confident, and make sure that your handshake is firm and your eye contact direct.

If the opposite is true and you are a very direct person and have dominance in your personality (Type A) and find the Type D (Compliant) or Type C (Measured) personalities difficult to deal with then you will need to force yourself to slow down. Take a more gentle approach, disguise your impatience, practise your listening skills and resist the temptation to prompt or interrupt. Make sure that your body language is not overpowering, and do not invade their personal space or you will appear intimidating.

If you err more to the Type D (Compliant) personality yourself then you will find it more difficult to sell to the Type A (Dominant) and the Type B (Social) personality but you should find it easier to sell to the Type C (Measured) personality. However, the danger here is that neither of you will want to close the sale. As the sales person you must take the initiative to close the sale so practise closing techniques with a colleague, or enrol on a sales course to help provide you with more confidence in this. As a Type D (Compliant) personality the key to becoming a successful sales person is by learning and following the sales structure, and practising it. Be attuned to others and be prepared to adapt your approach.

And if you are more of a Type B (Social) personality then you will need to make sure that your enthusiasm doesn't overpower the Type C (Measured) and Type D (Compliant) personalities. Slow down, be patient, provide the detail. And with the Type A (Dominant) personality you will need to cut out the social chit-chat, and be more businesslike and brisk.

It is not always possible to know beforehand the type of personality your prospective customer is going to be. From the beginning of the sales visit you should be looking for the body language signs and other indications that can give you clues as to the type of personality you are dealing with and then adapt your approach. This comes with practice, and with having an awareness of other people.

Q: I'm fine with the first part of the sales interview: the approach, discussion and diagnosis stages but then I seem to lose track and get stuck, why?

A: If you have successfully diagnosed which feature and benefit the prospective customer would respond to then you need to present this to them. It's possible that you are waiting for the customer to ask you a question or to take the initiative, which he won't. Or perhaps you are waiting for him to place the order. Again, he won't. It is far more likely that he'll say he'll think about it.

> You need to help the customer to buy.

Once you have diagnosed what the prospective customer needs then try summarising this. Summarising skills are essential for the successful sales person. It also confirms to the prospective customer that you have understood his business and/or his requirements. It demonstrates you have been listening. Don't worry if you have misunderstood, that's what summarising skills are for – to check that you have got all the information you need, and you have interpreted his needs correctly. If you haven't, the prospective customer will tell you and provide you with even more information, which can help you identify the correct features and benefits to present.

If you feel unable to summarise then check if you have asked enough open questions to fully understand what it is the customer needs or wants. You might think you have conducted the discussion stage of the interview adequately enough but perhaps you haven't.

Don't be nervous of asking lots of questions in the face-to-face sales interview, people love to talk about themselves and their business, and once you get someone talking you will just need to chip in with the occasional question to keep them on track. I can spend an hour on the discussion phase alone of the sales interview before moving on to other stages, even when someone has told me right at the beginning of the sales interview they can only give me 10 minutes. At the end of the sales interview (having won the sale I might add) the prospective customer is often surprised that he has been talking for so long!

Once you have summarised (and the prospective customer is agreeing with you) you must go straight in with presenting your products or services. Watch the body language of the prospective customer while you are presenting your features and benefits – is it participative and interested or still sceptical and distant? If the latter then ask him an open question to determine what it is that he's uneasy about, get any objections or questions aired. Answer these honestly and sincerely, check the customer is happy and then ask for the business by moving straight into closing. If he asks another question, or raises another objection, probe until you uncover what the real obstacle is and try and provide a compensating benefit to overcome it.

In summary, practise summarising, presenting your features and benefits and then trying to close.

Q: I've had a run of sales interviews now where I haven't won the order and I'm losing my confidence. What can I do?

A:It is important that you go into the sales interview with the right mental attitude and that is a positive one. What I suspect is that having lost some sales you are now going into the interview with a negative and nervous attitude, which in turn breeds yet more negativity. There is a saying, 'Adults fail because they expect to fail.' If you think you are going to fail then you almost certainly will. The danger is that your concern, nervousness and negativity will show through in your body language and the prospective customer will pick up on this. This in turn doesn't inspire him with confidence in you or your products or services. As a result he will be able to control the interview and steer it the way he wants rather than the way you want, and that is to a successful close. It is important that you drive the sales interview and that you stay in control of it. Having a positive attitude therefore is essential.

Here is how you can gain and maintain this positive attitude:

1. Hear the negative dialogue that is running through your mind before you go into a sales interview.

Are you saying something like this:

'I'm dreading this sales interview.'

'I just know I'll lose it like all the rest.'

'I'm useless at this.'

'I just know I won't be able to get the order.'

2. Recognise it for what it is, ie negative.

Examine all those statements above. They are all negative. If you go into a sales interview or make a telephone sales call with this kind of dialogue running through your mind then you are bound to lose the sale.

3. Challenge it.

How do you know you will lose this sale, you haven't even begun it yet? Have you lost every single sale you've ever approached? Are you *really* useless at it? Think about the sales successes you've had. How do you *know* you won't be able to get the order? Are you blessed with second sight?

4. Change it.

Having challenged the validity of your negative statements now change them to positive ones:

'I'm dreading this sales interview.'

Change to:

'I'm really looking forward to this sales interview. I can learn new things about this person and his company. I can really help this person by offering him my products.'

'I just know I'll lose it like all the rest.'

Change to:

'I feel confident about this opportunity. I am confident I can win this order.'

'I'm useless at this.'

Change to:

'I know my products thoroughly. I know the benefits they can bring to a company/person. I've got a great product and I will enjoy finding out about the prospective customer and seeing if my products/services can help him.'

'I just know I won't be able to get the order.'

Change to:

'I'm going to win this order. I have great products/services. I am confident. I can do it.'

TOP TIPS

Gaining and maintaining a positive attitude

- Hear the negative voice
- Recognise it
- Challenge it
- Change it

Tell yourself several times a day, and certainly before you go into a sales interview or make a telephone sales call, that you *can* win the business.

A positive inner dialogue sends positive signals to your body language

↓

Your positive body language sends even more positive signals back to your brain

↓

You *feel* more positive and confident

↓

You begin to act more positively and confidently

↓

The prospective customer *sees* more confident body language and *responds* to this positively

Tell yourself you have a great product or service and that you genuinely want to help other people by selling them something that will make their life more successful, easier or save them time etc.

Be enthusiastic, act enthusiastically and you will become enthusiastic. Don't let your own self-criticism, and other people's, drag you down. Believe you can do it and you will do it!

Q: I operate in a very competitive market. This means that my prospective customers will quite often say before they make a decision they want to see what my competitors have to offer. How should I handle this situation?

A:Welcome this objection and be confident that what you have to offer is better than your competitors. It is only natural for people to shop around, we all do it so why shouldn't your prospective customers?

You can quite openly acknowledge that the prospective customer is right to see what others have to offer. You can even mention your competitors yourself and praise one or two of them if you know they are reliable and trustworthy companies with good products to offer, knowing that what you have to offer is better, or better suits the prospective customer. Always be honest though and never knock the competition, it is unprofessional.

If the prospective customer is holding a beauty parade, ie inviting several companies to pitch for his business, try and establish who the others are and research them thoroughly before presenting yourself. Determine where in the presentation list you will be. If you are one of the first companies to present to the prospective customer, always try to go back to see the prospective customer after he has seen the others.

Acknowledge he is wise to consider others to see what they have to offer, ask when he is likely to have finished the process of selection, and get a guarantee that he will come back to you before making a final decision. You should try to arrange the interview after the first visit and before leaving if possible.

For example:

Sales person: 'I understand that you need to see others before making your decision, I would do the same if it were me **(acknowledge he is wise to do this).** What timeframe are you looking at?'

(Open question)

Prospective customer: 'I hope to have completed the process within the next month.'

Sales person: 'Great. I would be very keen to do business with you. So if you would allow me to come back with some proposals before you make your final decision, I'm sure I can come up with something that suits you. How about fixing a date for the beginning of May, when you've seen everyone? When would suit you best? Morning or afternoon?' **(Closing with the alternative close)**

CHAPTER 16

Checklists

CHECKLIST: COMMON MISTAKES OF SALES PEOPLE

- Lack of preparation. This includes lack of product/service knowledge.
- No knowledge and understanding of the features and benefits.
- Misjudging the decision maker and completely ignoring the other parties in the sales process.
- Poor grooming – sloppy and/or inappropriate for the target audience.
- Likes to talk and usually about themselves and their products/services.
- Opens up the conversation with his spiel and sticks to it.
- Doesn't ask open questions.
- Poor summarising skills – just carries on with his sales spiel.
- Overuse of prospective customer's name – insincere.
- Doesn't listen and can't answer the questions the prospective customer is asking.
- Is patronising – misjudges the level of communication.
- Ignores the objections or treats them defensively. Then starts to preach to the prospective customer.
- Won't take no for an answer!

CHECKLIST: WHAT MAKES A GOOD SALES PERSON

- Is genuine and sincere.
- Knows his products well, both their features and benefits.
- Is interested in people.
- Listens and asks open questions.
- Uses silences to good effect.
- Treats objections sincerely and the prospect as an intelligent, interesting individual.
- Helps people to buy by closing effectively.
- Always leaves on a positive note.

A TELEPHONE SALES CALL STRUCTURE:

Before making the call make sure you have:

A list of your features and benefits.

A list of the open questions: 'who', 'what', 'where', 'when', 'how' and 'why'.

A list of your situation questions.

Objective of the call:

Write down the objective for your call. What are you hoping to achieve?

APPROACH

Verbal handshake/ Introduction

How are you going to introduce yourself? Give your name, where you're from, and what you do. Be succinct.

Opening attention question

Start with an opening attention question to get the prospective customer talking.

DISCUSSION

Ask open situation questions

Don't ask too many or the prospective customer will become bored and restless and switch off.

DIAGNOSIS

Ask problem and needs questions

Try and identify what their problems and needs are.

Ask how satisfied are they with their current suppliers or services or what sort of difficulties they face.

IMPLICATIONS

Can you then identify the implications of these problems?

NEEDS

Summarise what they need and bring in the relevant features and benefits to fulfil that need or help solve their problem.

Finally...

Ask for an appointment, the order or the sale by using one of the closing techniques.

THE FACE-TO- FACE SALES INTERVIEW STRUCTURE

APPROACH

Arrive at the appointment early and take note of your surroundings, gather or look for any information that will help you during the sales interview.
Check your appearance and body language.
Introduce yourself.
Set the tone by making general opening remarks.
Adapt your approach to the type of personality you are selling to.

DISCUSSION

Ask open situation questions to stimulate discussion.
Listen intently to the answers and throughout the sales interview.

DIAGNOSIS

Ask problem or needs questions – try to uncover their needs.
Use comparative questions.

IMPLICATIONS

Use summarising skills to show you have understood and interpreted the implications of their problems and identified with their needs.

NEEDS

Tell them what they need by selling in the relevant feature and benefit which will help them to solve their problems/fulfil their needs.

QUESTIONS AND OBJECTIONS

Answer questions and handle objections.

CLOSE

Ask for the business or close the sale using the most appropriate closing technique.

CHANGE THE SUBJECT AND LEAVE

Index

JAICO PUBLISHING HOUSE

Elevate Your Life. Transform Your World.

ESTABLISHED IN 1946, Jaico Publishing House is home to world-transforming authors such as Sri Sri Paramahansa Yogananda, Osho, The Dalai Lama, Sri Sri Ravi Shankar, Robin Sharma, Deepak Chopra, Jack Canfield, Eknath Easwaran, Devdutt Pattanaik, Khushwant Singh, John Maxwell, Brian Tracy and Stephen Hawking.

Our late founder Mr. Jaman Shah first established Jaico as a book distribution company. Sensing that independence was around the corner, he aptly named his company Jaico ('Jai' means victory in Hindi). In order to service the significant demand for affordable books in a developing nation, Mr. Shah initiated Jaico's own publications. Jaico was India's first publisher of paperback books in the English language.

While self-help, religion and philosophy, mind/body/spirit, and business titles form the cornerstone of our non-fiction list, we publish an exciting range of travel, current affairs, biography, and popular science books as well. Our renewed focus on popular fiction is evident in our new titles by a host of fresh young talent from India and abroad. Jaico's recently established Translations Division translates selected English content into nine regional languages.

Jaico's Higher Education Division (HED) is recognized for its student-friendly textbooks in Business Management and Engineering which are in use countrywide.

In addition to being a publisher and distributor of its own titles, Jaico is a major national distributor of books of leading international and Indian publishers. With its headquarters in Mumbai, Jaico has branches and sales offices in Ahmedabad, Bangalore, Bhopal, Bhubaneswar, Chennai, Delhi, Hyderabad, Kolkata and Lucknow.

SINCE 1946